Spiritual Reflections
on the Sunday Gospels, **Cycle A**

To
Prais
To
Bless,
To
Preach

Peter John Cameron, O.P.

Our Sunday Visitor Publishing Division
Our Sunday Visitor, Inc.
Huntington, Indiana 46750

Nihil Obstat:

Francis J. McAree, S.T.D.
Censor Librorum

Imprimatur:

✠ Robert A. Brucato, D.D.
Vicar General, Archdiocese of New York
March 6, 2001

The Nihil Obstat and Imprimatur are official declarations that a book or pamphlet is free of doctrinal or moral error. No implication is contained therein that those who have granted the Nihil Obstat and Imprimatur agree with the contents, opinions, or statements expressed.

Our Sunday Visitor Publishing Division
Our Sunday Visitor, Inc.
200 Noll Plaza
Huntington, IN 46750

ISBN: 0-87973-824-3
LCCCN: 2001-131195

Cover design by Rebecca Heaston

PRINTED IN THE UNITED STATES OF AMERICA

In loving memory of my godparents
John and Sylvia Cummings

,

TABLE OF CONTENTS

PART ONE: REFLECTIONS ON THE SUNDAY GOSPELS

PART TWO: REFLECTIONS ON SOLEMNITIES AND ALSO FEASTS THAT MAY FALL ON SUNDAY

PREFACE

I have always taken consolation in a statement by St. Paul: "We write you nothing but what you can read and understand" (2 Cor 1:13). Sacred Scripture is intended to be intelligible. It is divine revelation, not obfuscation. The Bible is meant to be read and understood, not just by Scripture scholars, but by all believers. However, sometimes those without academic expertise in biblical studies get intimidated at the prospect of reading and interpreting the Word of God. The purpose of this book is to help Christians learn how to read and think about Sacred Scripture so as to unlock the power of the living Word of God — that is, to *actualize* the Gospel in their lives.

Like all great literature, Sacred Scripture is rich in allusions designed to deepen the readers' comprehension of the written message and to intensify their experience of the person of the author. Accordingly, Sacred Scripture possesses an organic, integral character. There is nothing merely casual, inadvertent, esoteric, or coincidental about Holy Writ. Rather, the Bible is a literary and theological masterpiece of divine and human intentionality. We "pierce the pearl" of the Word of God when we get to the heart of the Bible's intentionality.

When it comes to the Gospels, the Evangelists wrote about actual historical events in the life of Jesus Christ, but they dealt with that material *theologically*. The Evangelists wrote as theologians, not as historians per se. Hence, the *literal* sense is only the beginning of the meaning of the Word of God.

Inhering within the literal sense is the threefold *spiritual* sense: the *allegorical* sense, which relates everything to its significance in Christ; the *moral* sense, which illumines and informs human conduct; and the *anagogical* sense, which reveals the significance of realities and events from the perspective of life after death. To read and understand Sacred Scripture means appreciating its theological character in order to reach the richness of the spiritual sense.

At the same time, we must not forget that the sacred authors' own literary artistry contributes integrally to the mediation of the saving meaning of the Bible. In graduate school, my playwriting professor used to say that "the right word is a fugitive worth pursuing." The sacred authors, writing under the divine inspiration of the Holy Spirit, knew and employed this principle.

There were as many synonyms, literary devices, and modes of linguistic expression available to ancient biblical authors as there are today to contemporary authors. And God granted each sacred writer unhampered freedom to develop and employ the literary method that best suited the author at work. We authentically interpret the Gospels when we get to the heart of the creative choices that each Evangelist made. By studying and appreciating an Evangelist's personal literary style, one gains access to Scripture's spiritual sense and to the supernatural power of the Gospel to transform our lives.

In short, united to the Church's Magisterium, we are to approach the Bible with the same sensitivity and astuteness that we would bring to the reading of any work of literature. If we can read, we can read the Bible.

Fellow preachers, please keep in mind that each entry in this book is not a homily per se, but rather a mini-theological synthesis that aims to serve as a germ for personalized homiletic elaboration and presentation. Accordingly, the book endeavors to fulfill a directive of Pope John Paul II: "At the level of personal appropriation, the hearing of the Word of God proclaimed must be well prepared in the souls of the faithful by an apt knowledge of Scripture and, where pastorally possible, by *special initiatives designed to deepen understanding of the biblical readings*, particularly those used on Sundays and holy days" (*Dies Domini*, 40).

I am deeply grateful to Catherine Kolpak and Ann Marie Martelli for their kind clerical assistance in preparing this book.

Peter John Cameron, O.P.
June 29, 2000
Solemnity of Sts. Peter and Paul

Introduction

The Saving Force of Preaching

We tend at times to forget the saving power inherent in Sacred Scripture. St. James puts it plainly in his letter: "[The Father] willed to give us birth by the word of truth. . . . Humbly welcome the word that has been planted in you and is able to save your souls" (Jas 1:18, 21). And yet, upon reflection, even on the natural plane we recognize the real effectiveness of words to move us and change us.

For example, if someone were to say to us, "You're not going to believe this" or "You'd better sit down" or "Guess what!" or "I don't know how to tell you this," the words alone would induce in us an emotional reaction. They galvanize us. Even though we have no idea what may follow in the ensuing conversation, the striking dynamism of these words arrests our attention, fills us with anticipation, and primes us to listen. These words create a receptivity and predisposition in us that might otherwise never exist apart from their instrumentality. The words make us respond and be responsive.

A case in point: Not long ago, the news featured the story of a man who walked onto a private plane and greeted the co-pilot with the words "Hi, Jack!" The salutation was picked up by a microphone and misinterpreted by those on the other end as "hijack." Consequently, police, the county sheriff's SWAT team, and the FBI descended en masse on the airport. The moral: Beware! Words (even apart from the author's/speaker's intentionality) have devastating power.

Christ's Saving Events Reach Us via Word

In a far more exalted and sanctifying way, the holy Word of God accomplishes the same in us. The eminent Scripture scholar Fr. Francis Martin has noted that the sacred words of Scripture create within us an inner capacity to receive the action of the Holy Spirit, who applies the saving events of Jesus Christ to our life right now. That recreating and salvific action of the Holy Spirit began at the Annunciation. Pope John Paul II wrote that "in Mary's faith at the Annunciation, an interior space was reopened within humanity which the eternal Father can fill 'with every spiritual blessing.' It is the space 'of the new and eternal covenant.' "

The words of the angel to the Blessed Virgin Mary create in humanity an interior space to receive the Word of God and to be filled with the salvation that flows from his blood. The *Catechism of the Catholic Church* (CCC) confirms that one of the principal ways that the Holy Spirit builds up the Body of Christ in charity is "by God's Word 'which is able to build you up' [Acts 20:32 (RSV)]" (798). Accordingly, God continues to personalize that interior space, that inner capacity of the Annunciation in each one of us, through our reading and hearing the Word of God.

All of us are offered salvation by the historical events of the life of Christ that culminate in the Paschal Mystery. However, Christ's ever-effective saving actions now transpire and reach us on the level of word. That is why the priest or deacon, after proclaiming the Gospel, prays, "May the words of the Gospel wipe away our sins." Gospel words are salutary because they re-actualize Gospel events.

THE WORD OF GOD: THE MEANS TO BELIEF

Thus, the Bible is not simply "about" God; rather, the Bible enacts God's divine operation. Scripture scholar Mario Masini points out that "to hold the Bible as only a message greatly impoverishes its reality. Instead, . . . Scripture renders possible an ineffable encounter with the Word of God in the reality of his divinity."

Fr. William Hill, O.P., explains that "the Scriptures initiate us into a dialogue with their own subject matter which is God in his saving activity." A 1999 document from the Congregation for the Clergy entitled *The Priest and the Third Christian Millennium* stresses that "the revealed Word, made present and actualized 'in' and 'through' the Church, is an instrument through which Christ acts in us with his Spirit. . . . In hearing the Word, the actual encounter with God himself calls to the heart of man and demands a decision which is not arrived at solely through intellectual knowledge but which requires conversion of heart." As Archbishop Mariano Magrassi comments: "Since it constantly receives life from the indwelling Spirit, the Word contains in itself the power to save. . . . It is not only truth; it is power. It not only teaches; it is at work in us. It not only shows us models to imitate; it causes us to act." One monastic rule sums it up with this assertion: "We drink salvation from Sacred Scripture."

To engage Sacred Scripture is to realize the dynamism of the Redemption. At the end of his Gospel, John the Evangelist declares, "These [signs] are written that you may believe that Jesus is the Christ, the Son of God, and that believing you may have life in his name" (Jn 20:31 [RSV]). Event has become word in order to ensure the salvific benefit of Christ's saving actions to all who interact with his living Word. St. John understood well that his Gospel was not simply *about* Jesus; it is the very means of effecting belief in him.

PREACHING AS SACRAMENTAL

For this reason, Cardinal Joseph Ratzinger asserts that "Jesus' preaching can be called 'sacramental.' His word contains in itself the reality of the Incarnation and the theme of the cross and the Resurrection. It is 'deed/ word' in this very profound sense, instructing the Church in the mutual dependence of preaching and the Eucharist, and in the mutual dependence, as well, on preaching and an authentic, living witness."

The Priest and the Third Christian Millennium underscores this forcefully:

> The Gospel preached by the Church is not just a message
> but a divine and life-giving experience for those who be-
> lieve, hear, receive, and obey the message. . . . The procla-
> mation of the Gospel by sacred ministers of the Church is,
> in a certain sense, a participation in the salvific character
> of the Word itself, not only because they speak of Christ,
> but because they proclaim the Gospel to their hearers with
> that power to call which comes from their participation in
> the consecration and mission of the Incarnate Word of God.

And, in his book *Sacred Reading: The Ancient Art of Lectio Divina*, Fr. Michael Casey, O.C.S.O., adds:

> Both Scripture and Church . . . are . . . mysterious means
> by which we come into direct contact with the power of

15

salvation. In other words, they are "sacraments" — using this term in the broad sense. The Scriptures and the Church do not merely inform us about God; they provide the means by which we become part of what we read about. The proclamation of salvation is interactive — to receive revelation is to participate in the mystery that is revealed. . . . The purpose of God's Word is to save all of us.

The fourteenth-century German Dominican priest and mystical author John Tauler commented on how the written/spoken word gives us access to the Word of God who dwells in our soul. This sacred symbiosis obliges believers to avail themselves often of the Word of God. In this regard, Tauler wrote: "Through the outer word that people hear, they attain to the inner word, which God speaks in the essence of the soul. If the outer man has been strengthened and directs itself according to the internal man, he must again enter into himself, perceive and listen to the eternal Word, and this hearing brings him to everlasting life."

The night before his death, Jesus expressed this in the form of a prayer to his Father for his disciples: "Consecrate them in the truth. Your word is truth" (Jn 17:17).

In the case of demons, the inverse of this remains true. The Word of God prevents the devil from gaining access to the internal man or woman. As the chief exorcist of Rome, Fr. Gabriele Amorth, observes: "Many times I have written that Satan is much more enraged when we take souls away from him through confession than when we take away bodies through exorcism. In fact, we cause the devil even greater rage by preaching, because faith sprouts from the Word of God."

The author of the Russian tale *The Way of a Pilgrim* illustrates this through a story about an army officer who was addicted to alcohol. Desperate to gain self-control in his life, the officer turned to a holy monk who instructed him to read the Gospels every day, counseling him with these words: "God's special power is present in the Gospel through his words. Even when you don't understand the Word of God, the demons do, and they tremble."

All of this fills us with renewed admiration for St. Peter, who once asked Jesus, "Master, to whom shall we go? You have the words of eternal life" (Jn 6:68). To be one with the Savior is to be united to his saving Word, and vice versa.

PART ONE:
REFLECTIONS ON THE
SUNDAY GOSPELS

First Sunday of Advent

Getting Carried Away This Advent
Matthew 24:37-44

Christmas is about salvation. Nothing reminds us so strikingly of this fact as does the allusion to Noah and the flood in today's Gospel — the first word of Advent. In the days of Noah, God became greatly displeased with his people because the desires of the human heart were nothing but evil (Gn 6:5). Sadly, little has changed since those days. How many of us live self-centered, compromised lives, disobedient and oblivious to God. Once again, God will save us from our corruption, not simply with a good and blameless man like Noah who walked with God, but with a good and blameless man who is God himself — Jesus Christ. Advent renews God's sanctifying call to walk with him.

Just as the people of that time awaited the coming of the floodwaters, this Advent we await "the coming of the Son of Man." Noah spent the first "advent" of salvation building and readying the ark according to God's revealed plan. In the same way, we are to ready our souls so as to make them a worthy dwelling place for Emmanuel. Blessed Isaac of Stella once wrote that "Christ dwells until the end of the ages in the tabernacle of the Church's faith. He will dwell forever in the knowledge and love of each faithful soul." Hence, Christ's warning to us: "You must be prepared!"

The floodwaters carried away all the self-absorbed sinners in Noah's day. But God gives us this sacred season so that we might get carried away in Advent with personal repentance and re-dedication to the holiness of God. That is the significance of the second image in the Gospel today. To persuade us to be watchful this Advent, Jesus compares himself to a thief.

A thief is a threat — someone universally loathed, feared, and avoided. Why would the Lord, even metaphorically, associate himself with such a one? Because no one is indifferent to a thief. At first report of a thief's presence, our heart races, our pulse quickens, and our eyes remain peeled. If we are not vigilant, the thief will carry away what we consider most dear. Apathy spells disaster.

The lurking of a thief reminds us of what is most precious in our life. And so we remain alert and attentive in order to protect our possessions, to secure our safety, and to stave off harmful surprise. The work of a thief can draw a neighborhood together, unifying those who formerly were strangers, getting them to talk, to communicate, to advise and encourage. If the thief were not about, we would take our life for granted.

No wonder Christ does not hesitate to identify himself with a thief. But the only thing this Thief seeks to steal is our hearts. We need not fear that the Thief will carry away what we love. Rather, he comes to carry us away with his love.

On her deathbed, St. Thérèse of Lisieux grasped this mystery:

> It's said in the Gospel that God will come like a Thief. He will come to steal me away very gently. Oh, how I'd love to aid the Thief! . . . I'm not afraid of the Thief. I see him in the distance, and I take good care not to call out: "Help! Thief!" On the contrary, I call to him, saying: "Over here, over here!"

The season of Advent is a graced time to steel ourselves so that nothing will steal away the joy of our living in Christ's enlivening light. Jesus the Thief comes to us this Advent, not to take anything from us, but to keep us from taking our life for granted.

Second Sunday of Advent

Production, Presumption, and Preparation
Matthew 3:1-12

One major difference between people today and people in the time of John the Baptist is that they were willing to go out of their way — literally — to "acknowledge their sins." Many people today have duped themselves into thinking that they do not need a Messiah. We have lost any pertinent sense of either peril or piety. Many find the notion of sin to be obsolete at worst and merely quaint at best. Any "spiritual" impetus in their lives remains ordered to self-glorification and self-indulgence.

Thus, we readily recognize the urgency of John the Baptist's preaching today — "Repent!" The *Catechism* teaches that the Word became flesh for us in order to save us by reconciling us with God and in order to be our model of holiness. Advent, then, calls us to embrace that reconciliation and to follow Christ our Exemplar.

However, if we spurn a spirit of repentance this Advent, we identify ourselves with the "brood of vipers." By calling the Pharisees and Sadducees a "brood of vipers," John the Baptist personally fulfills the prophecy of Isaiah: he is the child who lays his hand on the adder's lair. At John's hand, we are called to heed the kingdom of heaven that is at hand. John shows us three practical aspects of repentance.

First, true repentance manifests itself in the production of good fruit. The outcome of self-giving love assures us that we are following the holy example of Jesus Christ. This is a key Gospel theme that Jesus himself will assert in his ministry (Mt 7:17, 19). It is too easy to kid ourselves about our conformity to Christ unless we and others can witness concrete evidence of our sanctity. At the same time, we need not rush our progress in holiness nor grow anxious over the coexistence of evil with goodness. The weeds may need to intermingle for a time with the wheat (Mt 13:24-30), but soon Christ will gather his wheat into the barn and burn the chaff.

Second, authentic repentance means living devoid of deadly presumption. How easily we deceive and delude ourselves through fleshly thinking and relativism, substituting a jejune deism for Gospel faith. St. Bernard pastorally warns: "If there is anyone who is not conscious of his defects, who is not very afraid of dangers, who does not fly devoutly for help to the newborn Salvation, who does not subject himself affectionately to God, such a one's adoration is not acceptable, his prostration is not true, his humility is of little worth, his faith will not be victorious for it is not lived."

And finally, the repentance validated by John's baptism is just the beginning. John's baptism prepares us for baptism with the Holy Spirit and fire. Yet, once we have recognized our sinfulness and repented of it, we still need to cultivate a humble, holy sense of our radical unworthiness apart from God, as John the Baptist himself does. However, we profess "I am not worthy" in a spirit of Gospel hope that the One who is coming will himself make us worthy by his coming. In fact, Christ defines worthiness as such confident reliance on the providence of God (Mt 10:9-10). In this spirit of hope, we personally prepare the way of the Lord by making straight the paths of our mind, our will, and our heart, and by offering ourselves completely to the baptizing power of the Holy Spirit. Accordingly, God responds by using people as unlikely as we — just as he used John the Baptist — to draw others to the Way, who is Jesus. We who are not worthy to carry Christ's sandals will soon be called to wash one another's feet.

THIRD SUNDAY OF ADVENT

JESUS OUR DESTINY
Matthew 11:2-11

The one thing that will console John the Baptist in prison is the assurance that Jesus is "the one who is to come." Even despite the harsh torment of incarceration, John remains focused, not on himself, but on Jesus. The Church teaches that the Word became flesh in order to make us partakers of the divine nature. Ravaged of his human rights and the personal dignity that is his due, John longs for a graced sharing in that divine nature. Such grace is the Baptist's only relief and solace.

That yearning explains why Jesus does not answer the question posed by the disciples of the Baptist today with a simple yes. Rather, the reply that the Lord sends back to John is both a confirmation of Christ's supernatural identity and an invitation to the seeker to share personally in it. Only God can restore sight to the blind, make the lame ambulatory, cleanse lepers, give hearing to the deaf, and raise the dead to life. Most importantly, only a loving God takes the initiative in proclaiming the Good News to the poor. The sign that Jesus is the One, the Messiah, is the fact that he prefers the suffering, the needy, the lowly, the lost, and the poor. He makes them the priority of his ministry. At the moment, John the Baptist himself is the poor one who has the Good News proclaimed to him.

In reality, through the question he poses, John the Baptist is seeking his destiny, who is Jesus Christ. Advent reminds us that Jesus Christ is our true destiny. For, as Msgr. Luigi Giussani, founder of the Communion and Liberation movement, has observed, "the desire to bend destiny to our own will always takes over. It is an urge to establish meaning and value as we would like them to be." Despite the excruciating horror and heartaches of life, any attempt to fulfill our happiness in something other than Jesus Christ is an exercise in frustration and futility. It causes us to spurn our God-given destiny. The more we seek solace in anything outside of Jesus, the more we impound ourselves in prisons of our own making.

The incomparable greatness of John the Baptist consists in his unfailing persistence in uniting himself to Jesus' presence wherever he is, whether it be in his mother's womb, in the desert, or in prison. Msgr. Giussani makes the point that the more we reflect without the light of faith on our destiny, the more we suffer from "the loneliness of bewilderment." As he explains, "Only the divine itself can adequately help the man who recognizes his existential impotence, that hidden divinity, the mystery which somehow becomes involved with man's trials, enlightening and sustaining him along his pathway." John the Baptist knows this truth and it fills him with joy. The mystery of Christ's divinity is meant to be the source of our joy as well on this Gaudete Sunday.

The Good News that John hears today liberates him, despite the physical impediment of prison bars. His condition encourages us that, when things are not going our way, if we seize God with our mind, the presence of the Gospel will transform us. C. S. Lewis once made the statement that God can show himself as he really is only to real people. John the Baptist is a "real person," disposed and primed — as in Jesus Christ we are called to be — to discover the revelation of God in the Incarnation of Jesus Christ. As one young man reflecting on his faith expressed it: "Everything depends on your attitude. If it is not humble and doesn't recognize reality — that is, God's presence — it makes your life superficial and does not let you get to the bottom of things." Getting to the bottom of things means finding the fullness of our destiny in Jesus Christ, who calls us by his birth and our rebirth to be partakers in the divine nature.

Fourth Sunday of Advent

Jesus' Heart, Mary's Hands, and Joseph's Home
Matthew 1:18-24

The Gospel does not tell us how Joseph learned that Mary was "with child," but we can presume that, at the news, all Joseph's plans and dreams were shattered — until he had the dream that changed his life. One school of scientific thought holds that we *need* to dream, because if we do not dream we might become insane. Today's Gospel episode drives home how much we need Joseph to have this dream in order to rescue us from the insanity of sin.

The *Catechism* teaches that "the Word became flesh *so that thus we might know God's love*" (458). The irony is that we come to know God's love in the Incarnation through Joseph's broken heart. One of the most difficult truths of the Gospel concerns the reprioritizing of love that Jesus demands: "Whoever loves father or mother more than me is not worthy of me" (Mt 10:37). Yet, Joseph demonstrates how worthy he is of God by sublimating whatever conflicting emotions he might feel as a result of his love for Mary, and by fulfilling the command of the angel out of undivided love for the Lord. As strange as it may seem, certain scientific studies attest that, after undergoing heart transplant surgery, many recipients have dreams about the donor. Through the abandonment of his broken heart to God, Joseph receives from the Divine Physician a new heart — the very heart of Jesus who fills his dreams and transforms his life.

The wholeness of faith that we witness in Joseph remains crucial for us in our final preparations for Christmas. Thomas Merton noted that "it is the *whole man* who either goes out to meet Christ in his Advent, or rejects him with indifference. . . . I begin to live to Christ when I come to the 'end' or to the 'limit' of what divides me from my fellow man: when I am willing to step beyond this end, cross the frontier, become a stranger, enter into the wilderness which is not 'myself' . . . where I am alone and defenseless in the desert of God." The Greek verb for *awaking* or *arising* is also used in the Gospel to refer to Christ's healing (Mt 8:15), the manifestation of his divine authority over nature (Mt 8:26), his power to forgive (Mt 9:5-7), and his transfiguring grace (Mt 17:7). In awakening from his sleep, Joseph steps beyond himself and meets God-with-us in the defenselessness of divine mystery. When we awake like Joseph enlivened by the confidence of faith, we embody the supernatural might of the Son of God. God blesses Joseph with the privilege of giving Jesus his name because Joseph lives by the redeeming name of Jesus.

In order to cross this frontier, Joseph must first permit Mary to cross his threshold as his wife. Thomas Merton also wrote that "the mystery can only be known by those who enter into it, who find their place in the Mystical Christ, and therefore find the mystery of Christ realized and fulfilled *in themselves.*" Joseph enters into this mystery and finds his place in Christ by letting Jesus enter his home in Mary his bride. St. Bernard tells us that "God did not wish us to have anything which had not passed through Mary's hands." By passing into his home as his beloved spouse, Mary realizes and fulfills in Joseph her husband all the graces of her divine Son that pass through her immaculate hands.

Joseph the just man prefigures the just who welcome Jesus when he is away from home (Mt 25:37). They testify how much they have come to know God's love in his incarnate Son by the magnanimous way that they show God's love to others. In reciprocity, at the Second Coming — the Final Advent — Christ the King will bless those just ones who emulate his foster-father Joseph and welcome them into the eternal home of heaven (Mt 25:34). In that welcome, all our dreams come true.

THE HOLY FAMILY

THE FORMULA FOR A HAPPY FAMILY
Matthew 2:13-15, 19-23

Perhaps the best way to understand the blessing of the Holy Family is to consider what our life would be like without any family. That deprivation would leave us in a state of utter loneliness. Jesus knows how much such solitariness terrifies us. That is why, the night before he dies, he reassures us that he will not leave us orphans (Jn 14:18). Cardinal Joseph Ratzinger observed that loneliness is "in fundamental contradiction with the nature of man, who cannot exist alone; he needs company. That is why loneliness is the region of fear, which is rooted in the exposure of a being that must exist but is pushed out into a situation which he cannot endure."

Herod finds himself in that region of fear. He cannot endure the situation of God incarnate in his midst. The presence of Jesus Christ only exacerbates the consuming loneliness wreaked by Herod's egoism. In order to insure that he continues to exist, Herod decides to end the existence of every male infant in his realm. In effect, Herod prefigures the modern mentality so intent on exterminating human families.

But doesn't the Gospel give mixed signals about the importance of family? In calling James and John, Jesus requires that they abandon their father (Mt 4:21-22). Moreover, Jesus reproves a would-be disciple who wants to bury his father before following (Mt 8:21-22). Christ also warns about the betrayals to take place between immediate family members (Mt 10:21, 35). The Lord goes so far as to declare that anyone who loves father, mother, son, or daughter more than him is not worthy of him (Mt 10:37).

But that is the key. In our love for Jesus Christ, all human loves are reordered, elevated, and consecrated. Via the primacy of our love for Jesus we receive the ability to love others in a sanctified way and, in turn, to generate the love of Christ, especially through the community of family. Jesus proclaims, "Whoever does the will of my heavenly Father is my brother, and sister, and mother" (Mt 12:50).

St. Joseph models the love of the Father's will that surpasses his own feelings or human affections. In Joseph's obedience to the Father's will, the greater holy family that Christ predicts begins to form. By heeding the counsel of the angel, Joseph not only saves his nuclear family but gains a much greater one (Mt 19:29). If we reverence the peace of God and dutifully love our enemies, we become sons of the heavenly Father (Mt 5:9, 45). The love and sanctity of the Holy Family are ordered to enabling all God's children to say "Our Father" (Mt 6:9; 23:9). The love of Jesus, Mary, and Joseph that leads us to the Father exterminates the loneliness that stalks us.

Blessed Jacobus de Voragine relates in *The Golden Legend* how the dying Herod was filled with spite when he learned that the Jews joyfully looked forward to his death. In retaliation, he arrested and imprisoned several young sons from the finest Jewish families, saying to his sister: "Well, I know that the Jews will rejoice at my death, but I foresee many of them grieving and many stately funerals if you carry out my wish: Just kill all those young Jews I hold in prison. Then all Judea will mourn over me, against their will though it be." So much for Herod's conception of a happy family.

Second Sunday After Christmas

Word, Light, Son
John 1:1-18

The *Catechism* teaches us that "the Son of God . . . communicates to his humanity his own personal mode of existence in the Trinity. In his soul as in his body, Christ thus expresses humanly the divine ways of the Trinity" (470). The Incarnation that we celebrate at Christmas is "the mystery of the wonderful union of the divine and human natures in the one person of the Word" (483). However, Christmas is also the celebration of our union with Jesus Christ and with the fullness of his own life that he came to impart. Our sharing in the mystery of the Incarnation enables us to express through lived faith the divine ways of the Blessed Trinity.

The evangelist John emphasizes three ways that Christ shares his life with us at Christmas. First of all, the Word of God, the Second Person of the Trinity, "was in the beginning with God" and is the one through whom "all things came to be . . . and without [the Word] nothing came to be." The Word is the very source of creation, the principle of life itself. In the gift of the humanity of Jesus, God invites us never to be apart from the re-creating power of his Son. In the Lord's visible flesh, we receive from heaven an infallible means to resist relying on ourselves and to enjoy unceasing access to life in all its newness.

Without faith-filled union with the Son, we risk coming to nothing. United with Jesus, all things — even those that seem fantastic or impossible — come to be. The more we meditate on that Word, the more we discover how the mortality of Christ engenders immortality in us.

Moreover, with the coming of Christ, "the true light which enlightens everyone" shines to dispel our personal darkness. Those who see his glory become beneficiaries of a life of hope. In his book on the nature and meaning of light, David Park writes: "Light is enfolded in our words, our habits, our mental image of the world, and as that image changes, light changes with it." Christ the light is not only enfolded into our words, habits, and images, but he envelops and perfects them. The light of Christ reveals us to ourselves in the fullness of our human dignity and vocation. The more that the light of Christ changes and perfects our image of self and the world, the more perfectly we see the unchanging grace and truth of Christ's light.

And finally, "to those who did accept him he gave power to become children of God." To accept Jesus Christ requires an act of love whereby our very identity becomes transformed. When we love Jesus, the Lord takes us up into his family as one of his own. To accept Jesus in heartfelt belief is to acquire a divine way of belonging. G. K. Chesterton once wrote: "It is said truly in a sense that Pan died because Christ was born. . . . Atheism is abnormality. It is not merely the denial of dogma. It is the reversal of a subconscious assumption in the soul: the sense that there is a meaning and a direction in the world it sees."

The deepest longings of our heart, which no mythology or idolatry can satisfy, are met in the One who, as soon as he can speak, will teach us to pray "Our Father." We receive the meaning and direction that we seek in the world in the fullness freely given of him who dwells among us. To love Jesus is to share in the glory of the Father's only Son as sons and daughters ourselves.

THE EPIPHANY OF THE LORD

ENLIGHTENMENT VS. EPIPHANY
Matthew 2:1-12

The fact that the Magi leave their country and follow a star in search of the newborn king of the Jews signals to us how much we, too, require an illumination outside of ourselves in order to appreciate and appropriate the mystery of the Incarnation. A common tendency nowadays is for people to think that they possess within themselves all the natural insight and knowledge needed to understand the world and to reach the meaning of life. The Enlightenment mentality taints us with a prideful intellectual superiority that leads us to regard our rational powers as supreme and infallible. It tempts us to rationalism and the presumption that we know better than God. It lures us into making an idol out of innate intelligence.

However, the *Catechism* makes very clear that all human beings stand "in need of being enlightened by God's revelation, not only about those things that exceed [human] understanding, but also 'about those religious and moral truths which of themselves are not beyond the grasp of human reason' " (38). Jesus Christ is the way that God has revealed his plan of loving goodness and given himself to his people. Therefore, the solemnity of the Epiphany calls us, like the Magi, to leave behind our preconceptions and to get beyond our own ideas so as to enter into the mystery manifested in the revelation of Jesus Christ. As Cardinal John Henry Newman once wrote, "The rationalist makes himself his own center, not his Maker; he does not go to God, but he implies that God must come to him." The Magi are wise men because they do not seek their own wisdom. Rather, they go to God.

We do not know the Magi's names, but their profession indicates that they are men of advanced education and learning. And yet, even though the otherwise anonymous Magi are presented to us by way of their scholarly expertise, their pilgrimage suggests that they are depending on something more than their wits. Theirs is a journey of hope. They place all their trust in the heavenly light that surpasses any of their own understanding or judgment.

The Magi obviously expect King Herod to welcome their intention of paying homage to God incarnate. Otherwise, they would have been more discreet about revealing their purpose to him. But for Herod, Christ's revelation only spells despair. Caught up in his own sinfulness, Herod spurns the light of divine revelation needed to clarify the reality of sin. And without the knowledge that divine revelation gives of God, neither Herod nor we cannot recognize sin clearly.

Conversely, the eschewal of self-love frees us to love God with the strength of his own ineffable wisdom. We see this demonstrated in the Magi as they prostrate themselves before the Christ child and do him homage. Their joy-filled love is expressed in living faith. The *Catechism* reminds us that faith is a "personal adherence" to God of the whole man involving "an assent of the intellect and will" to the self-revelation of God (176). One of the most common yet hidden temptations in the life of faith is a lack of faith that, the *Catechism* tells us, "expresses itself less by declared incredulity than by our actual preferences" (2732). Epiphany is a time to join the Magi in manifesting our actual preference to live only for God.

The elucidation of faith that surpasses mere human enlightenment transforms even the unconscious of the Magi. As they depart for their country by another way, they will never obey any other voice than the one that graced and fulfilled their greatest dreams.

THE BAPTISM OF THE LORD

BAPTISM AS REGENERATION
Matthew 3:13-17

One reason that Jesus comes to John at the Jordan to be baptized is to show us that our attempts at happiness are bound to fail if they are not rooted in God the Father's love. For private efforts at self-fulfillment are essentially the work of the sin of pride. And pride, like all sin, is a rejection of the Father's love in favor of self-directed pleasure and ambition.

The Baptism of the Lord reveals how much Jesus understands our plight and identifies with it. He knows that, without the love of the Father animating our life, we are plunged into anger, selfishness, jealousy, greed, arrogance, pettiness, lust, apathy, violence, etc. That is why Jesus tells John the Baptist to "allow it for now" — that is, to plunge him in the waters of the river in baptism. That sacred action signifies three important graces for us.

First of all, the baptism of Jesus underscores the way that we come to participate in the favor of the Father. The abandonment of Christ before the Baptist stands as the model for our sanctification. For in the act of acknowledging our sinfulness by obediently submitting ourselves to the providence of grace, the Father fulfills our need for redemption. Accordingly, baptism is a kind of self-surrender that results in re-creation. In the encyclical *Veritatis Splendor*, Pope John Paul II asserts that "we are in a certain way our own parents, creating ourselves as we will by our decisions" (71). Just as John the Baptist "allowed" Jesus to be baptized, so do we experience the recreating power of the Spirit of God coming upon us when we allow Providence to direct our life. We act as our own parents when we confess our powerlessness apart from reliance on God's providence.

Moreover, the self-surrender of baptism is tantamount to death. Msgr. Luigi Giussani has written that "baptism, as the place where the Mystery dies inside human evil and rises by the divine power that it has within it, is the place where belonging to God acquires from God himself a super-

35

nature, a nature that is greater." We revitalize this belonging and this sharing in the divine nature every time we renew our baptismal promises. Our assent to the questions — "Do you reject Satan? And all his works? And all his empty promises?" — constitutes a real dying to the exaltation of self that is the central element in Satanism. In our experience of dying to sinfulness, the Father communicates his love and favor with resurrectional force.

And finally, baptism is an act of spiritual regeneration. The voice of the Father that comes from the heavens — "This is my beloved Son, with whom I am well pleased" — continues to resound in our own ears as it generates the Father's own life in us from moment to moment. The Baptism of the Lord reveals that the Father's love is the only thing that can make us happy and satisfy us ultimately in life. The more that we share mystically in the Mystery that dies in human evil, the more does the delusion of evil die out in us, giving rise to nothing less than sonship and daughtership with Christ, which is what it means to live.

SECOND SUNDAY IN ORDINARY TIME

BEHOLD
John 1:29-34

This is one of those rare Gospels in which Jesus says absolutely nothing. And yet, how powerfully the Word among us transforms us. John the Baptist sees and testifies to this today. John has come so that Jesus "might be made known." The Baptist begins the showing, the revealing that unfolds to a climax in the Gospel of John. Jesus' first miraculous sign at Cana reveals his glory and engenders belief in his disciples (Jn 2:11). In the same way, Jesus heals the man born blind so that God's works would show forth in him (Jn 9:3). Before his death, Jesus attests to the Father that he has revealed the Father's name to his disciples (Jn 17:6). And after the Resurrection, Jesus shows himself to his disciples (Jn 21:1, 14).

In other words, John the Baptist wants us to see what he himself has come to recognize in the Lamb of God. That is why he commands us, "Behold!" John's entreaty is an invitation to the mercy that flows from the One who takes away the sin of the world. This beholding will ready us to obey Jesus on the night before he dies when he will warn us, "Behold, the hour is coming . . . when each of you will be scattered" (Jn 16:32). We will hear the antithesis of John's invitation to compassion on the lips of Pilate when he demands, "Behold, the man!" and "Behold, your king!" (Jn 19:5, 14) in order to provoke the crowd's condemnation of Christ. What preserves us from joining our voice to the crucifying crowd is our moral conformity to Jesus. For this reason, at the foot of the cross we are privileged to behold Mary as our mother and ourselves as children of the Mother of God (Jn 19:26-27).

Like the crowd calling for Christ's crucifixion, we too will reject Christ's kingship if we misunderstand its purpose. As the Baptist insists, this is the Lamb of God who takes away the sin of the world. Jesus himself will stress the insidiousness of sin (Jn 8:21, 24, 34, 46; 15:22, 24; 16:8, 9; 19:11). However, as the fifth-century bishop Diadochus of Photice once wrote, the trouble is that "very few people can accurately recognize all their own faults; indeed, only those can do this whose intellect is never torn away from the remembrance of God."

Jesus takes away our sin so that we will never be torn away from a recollected remembrance of God. It begins when Jesus orders the merchants selling doves in the temple to take them away (Jn 2:16). Upon curing him, Jesus tells the lame man to take away his mat (Jn 5:9). And Christ commands those attending to take away the stone from Lazarus' tomb (Jn 11:39, 41). In other words, the merciful authority of Jesus Christ takes away everything that is blasphemous, crippling, and obstructive to the fullness of life in him. Mary Magdalene frets that a thief has come and taken away the body of Jesus (Jn 20:13, 15). But just as Jesus affirms that his disciples will not be taken out of the world (Jn 17:15), neither can he be removed. Rather, he blesses his faithful ones with a joy that no one can take from them (Jn 16:22), and he invests them with his own divine power to take away sins (Jn 20:23). In this way, our remembrance of God remains holy and the recognition of our sins accurate.

The Spirit of Truth who remains with us (Jn 14:17) assures the Baptist that the man coming toward him is the Lamb of God. And just as the Spirit remains with Jesus, so are we to remain in Jesus (Jn 6:56; 15:4-7). The Word of the Father will not remain in those who refuse to believe (Jn 5:38). Rather, the wrath of God remains with those who disobey the Son (Jn 3:36). But John's obedience and hope lead him to proclaim the words that we hear the priest proclaim at Mass: "Behold, the Lamb of God!" We rejoice that Jesus ranks ahead of us in every way, for then we can pray with confidence: "Lamb of God, you take away the sins of the world, have mercy on us . . . grant us peace."

Third Sunday in Ordinary Time

St. Joseph: Exemplar of the Ministry of Jesus
Matthew 4:12-23

Whenever Jesus "withdraws" in the Gospel of Matthew, he does so to avert a hindrance threatening his ministry so as to gain new focus and intensity for that ministry (Mt 12:15; 14:13; 15:21). Moreover, the Magi withdraw to their own country by another route in order to safeguard what they have received through their encounter with the incarnate Christ (Mt 2:12-13); and twice, St. Joseph, under angelic inspiration, withdraws with his family in order to protect his family (Mt 2:14, 22). Only disbelieving mourners (Mt 9:24) and the deceitful Judas (Mt 27:5) withdraw as a result of their faithlessness. All of this means that "withdrawing" in the Gospel of Matthew is an invitation to more perfect faith.

Further emphasis is placed on this action of Jesus when we are told that he "went to live" in Capernaum. In this, Jesus imitates both Joseph who settles in Nazareth (Mt 2:23) and God who dwells in the temple (Mt 23:21). At the same time, this settling pertains to the seven evil spirits who take up residence in a newly tidied soul (Mt 12:45). In other words, the Gospel's invitation to a more profound faith calls us to examine spiritually "where we live" and who dwells in us — God or the devil. That is why repentance is the keynote of this passage and of the whole of the Gospel.

The first thing Jesus does when he moves into his new neighborhood is to seek out his companion disciples. Responding to the summons "Come after me" is not a one-time matter. Rather, it requires constant conversion: "Whoever loves father or mother more than me is not worthy of me, and whoever loves son or daughter more than me is not worthy of me; and whoever does not take up his cross and follow after me is not worthy of me" (Mt 10:37-38). This imperative even accompanies Christ's prediction of his Passion: "Whoever wishes to come after me must deny himself, take up his cross, and follow me" (Mt 16:24).

No wonder, then, that Matthew tells us that James and John "left their boat *and their father* and followed him" (Mt 4:22). There can be no exceptions to total abandonment to Christ — not the burying of one's father (Mt 8:21) or even betrayal by one's father (Mt 10:21). We have one Father in heaven (Mt 23:9) who, in Christ, calls us to do his will without vacillation (Mt 21:31). For to see Jesus in all people and in every circumstance makes us blessed by the Father and gains us a share in the kingdom of heaven that Christ proclaims today (Mt 25:34).

What Jesus demands of his disciples he has undertaken himself. Jesus has withdrawn from the security of his family home. No longer does he live within easy reach of parental support and encouragement, but within the very providence of God. The people know Jesus to be the son of Joseph the carpenter (Mt 1:16; 13:55), and they recognize that he himself has "abandoned" his foster-father's profession in order to serve the one Father. Jesus today emulates the holy obedience of St. Joseph in his withdrawing, his living, and his drawing others into the life of the Father. In a powerful way, Joseph's consecrated life serves as the exemplar for Christ's earthly ministry.

To those who respond — "those dwelling in a land overshadowed by death" — the gift of the Father will be given in all its transfiguring fullness. For the ones today who faithfully follow Jesus will experience the overshadowing of a bright cloud from which comes the voice of the Father promising, "This is my beloved Son" (Mt 17:5).

FOURTH SUNDAY IN ORDINARY TIME

THE BLESSEDNESS OF JESUS
Matthew 5:1-12a

What anticipation of great promise must have prompted the crowds to make the arduous ascent to the top of the mountain. Were they disappointed upon arrival to learn just how unglamorous the blessed really are?

The poor in spirit enjoy their predilection for beatitude since they are receptive to the preaching of the Good News (Mt 11:5) and keenly reliant upon the goodness of Jesus (Mt 19:21). Likewise, those who mourn have first rejoiced in the presence of the Bridegroom (Mt 9:15). Their mourning expresses their yearning for the Bridegroom. Moreover, the meek inherit the land because they are obedient to the Lord to the point of being conformed to his model of meekness (Mt 11:29).

Those who hunger and thirst for righteousness are satisfied with a holiness that surpasses the superficiality of the Pharisees (Mt 5:20; 6:1; 12:1, 3; 23:23). Christ's own hungering becomes an occasion for receiving a windfall of faith (Mt 21:18-22). It is the hunger and thirst for righteousness that moves the "sheep" to tend to the hungry and thirsty in their midst (Mt 25:35, 37, 46). All those who seek first the righteousness of God (Mt 6:33) like John the Baptist (Mt 3:15) — who, on his diet of locusts and wild honey, truly must have been hungry and thirsty (Mt 3:4) — receive a satisfaction opposite to the one the world would presume (Mt 21:32).

The merciful are blessed because they devote themselves to Christ's desire for mercy (Mt 9:13; 12:7) by imitating his unceasing offer of mercy (Mt 9:27; 15:22; 17:15; 18:33; 20:30-31). In the same way, the clean of heart have purified themselves of the compromise and deception of the scribes and Pharisees who cleanse only the outside (Mt 23:25-26). By condoning the loot and lust that remain within them, they are more in need of cleaning than the lepers whom Jesus cures (Mt 8:2-3; 10:8; 11:5).

The peacemakers are blessed because they are the ones who take up Christ's commission to proclaim the Kingdom (Mt 10:13) and who embrace the truth that Gospel peace is the fruit of the Lord's new order that overturns the world (Mt 10:34).

The persecuted are blessed because the experience of persecution provides an incomparable opportunity to witness to the efficacy of Gospel charity (Mt 5:44), because they allow the seed of the Word to take root (Mt 13:21), and because they abandon themselves to the will of God for ushering in the fulfillment of the Kingdom (Mt 23:34). Similarly, the insulted are blessed because they are deeply configured to Jesus, who on the cross suffered the insults and mocking of so many false accusers (Mt 27:39-44).

However, the greatest verification that the Beatitudes are true is the fact that Jesus fulfills them himself. He begins his life in the poverty of the manger. He mourns publicly at the death of Lazarus. He calls himself meek as if it were a title (Mt 21:5). He hungers in the desert in his time of temptation, and he thirsts on the cross. His mercy extends even to the bestowal of forgiveness to his crucifiers. The cleanness of his heart is revealed through the opening in his pierced side. "Peace" is his first word of greeting after the Resurrection. The persecution of his Passion and the insults of Calvary remain his great trophies. No wonder that those whom Christ declares blessed are, in the eyes of the world, as little deserving of a reward as the workers hired late were deserving of their generous wages — the Greek word for *reward* and *wages* is the same (Mt 20:8).

FIFTH SUNDAY IN ORDINARY TIME

SALT AND LIGHT
Matthew 5:13-16

Jesus Christ reveals us to ourselves, and he does so in a pointed way today as he calls us "salt" and "light." Both images signify that, by our covenantal relationship with Jesus Christ, Christians can mediate a transformative effect on the world. In fact, the vocation of humanity is to show forth the image of God. However, it is altogether possible for salt to become insipid and for light to mask its radiance. This Gospel, then, is about allowing God to actualize the ultimate potential in us. We do so by living to the full the relationship with the only One who can make us and keep us salty and shiny to the glory of God.

The Christian's ability to season the world, to preserve it, and to purify it like salt remains the direct result of union with Jesus Christ. No wonder, then, that salt which loses its taste suffers the harsh penalty of being "thrown out." In this regard, the tasteless salt is like the fruitless tree (Mt 3:10), the tree that bears bad fruit (Mt 7:19), the eye and the hand that cause trouble (Mt 5:29-30; 18:8-9), the short-lived grass (Mt 6:30), apostates (Mt 13:42), the useless (Mt 13:48), and the wicked (Mt 13:50). In fact, the expression to "lose taste" is synonymous with "foolishness" — the kind of foolishness we see in the one who hears Christ's words but does not put them into practice (Mt 7:26), the blind scribes and Pharisees (Mt 23:17), and the five foolish virgins (Mt 25:2-3, 8). Unlike the holiness that becomes our own through union with Jesus, tasteless salt deserves to be trampled underfoot (Mt 7:6).

Similarly, Christians conformed to Christ the Light of the World become light of the world. Christians radiate the light announced at the outset of Christ's ministry (Mt 4:16) through the lamp of the eye (Mt 6:22-23). Our conformity to Christ compels us also to speak in the light (Mt 10:27). In this way, Christians come to share personally in the resplendence of the Transfiguration, whose light the apostles glimpse on the mountaintop (Mt 17:2, 5).

Accordingly, like the transfigured Christ, Christians' light must dazzle others. More specifically, our communion with Christ sanctifies us so that we will shine like the sun in the Father's kingdom (Mt 13:43). For through the illumination of our unhidden light, others are able to see our good deeds to the glory of God. Unlike the self-seeking scribes and Pharisees who go out of their way to perform religious deeds publicly in order to be noticed, our good deeds are good precisely because they are motivated by the Father's love and they serve the Son, like the woman who anoints Jesus before his death (Mt 26:10).

The supernatural essence of this light is disclosed in the fact that people will glorify God, and not us, for the goodness they witness in us. Here again the Pharisees fail. When they see Jesus casting out demons, the Pharisees presume Christ's ability to effect such goodness proceeds from an alliance with the Evil One (Mt 9:34; 12:24). However, when others permit the light of the Gospel to penetrate the darkness of their hearts, they will correctly attribute the genuine holiness viewed in us to the cause of that holiness: our heavenly Father. Then, like the crowds at the healing of the paralytic (Mt 9:8) and of the many sick on the mountainside (Mt 15:31), they will glorify God. For they will realize that, left to ourselves, not only would we be tasteless and lightless, we would be more paralyzed, crippled, deformed, blind, and mute than the throngs that Jesus heals.

SIXTH SUNDAY IN ORDINARY TIME

THE BEATITUDES IN ACTION
Matthew 5:17-37

Christ's goal is to bring to fulfillment in himself everything that has already been revealed, "the law and the prophets." That is why today he enjoins us to a life of virtue characterized by obedience, fidelity, charity, mercy and reconciliation, purity, self-giving, constancy, truthfulness, and integrity.

The commandments that Jesus explicates today are in fact fulfilled in living out the Beatitudes that he has just proclaimed (Mt 5:1-12).

"Blessed are the poor in spirit." That poverty extends even to living spiritually without an eye or a hand if either "causes you to sin." Poverty of spirit requires that kind of radical detachment from anything that would commit us to Gehenna and keep us from the paradise of heaven.

"Blessed are they who mourn." Among the sorrowing are those suffering from the affront of another. The experience of mourning reveals just how deep is the need for reconciliation and how important it is for the one offended – the mourner – to initiate that reconciliation. The consolation that attends such magnanimous self-emptying is the graced ability to worship worthily at the altar of salvation.

"Blessed are the meek." Chief among the meek are those lowly enough to put aside their own ideas, opinions, presuppositions, and prejudices and to accept docilely the commandments of God in all their fullness. For those who are dedicated to the Law of God, greatness is not earthly or self-made. Rather, those who live obedient to the commandments are "called greatest in the kingdom of heaven."

"Blessed are they who hunger and thirst for righteousness." Hunger, like sincerity, is usually self-evident; it does not require convincing or histrionics. In the same way, those who hunger and thirst for holiness are forthright, candid, earnest people. Their "yes" means "yes," and their "no" means "no." In fact, to live in repudiation of such simple resoluteness is the very opposite of hungering after holiness: "Anything more is from the evil one."

"Blessed are the merciful." How easy it is to turn our backs on mercy and to let anger dominate our life. Yet, if we exhibit anger toward our brothers or sisters, we become "liable to judgment," where we can expect a similar lack of mercy. If we stoop to calling another "you fool," we will be the first to feel the stupidity of our own foolishness. However, to live mercifully makes us answerable, not to the Sanhedrin, but to the very mercy of Jesus.

"Blessed are the clean of heart." The pure of heart are those sensitive enough to realize how easy it is to commit adultery in one's heart. The clean of heart shall see God because they look for God whenever they look upon their neighbor. That holy regard frees us from the snares of lust and from the temptation to turn other persons into sexual objects.

"Blessed are the peacemakers." Peacemakers possess the prudence to settle quickly with their opponents. For they know that no court can bestow the privilege of being children of God. Only the self-exercise of divine peace achieves that.

"Blessed are they who are persecuted for the sake of righteousness." This includes those who teach the commandments with righteousness that "surpasses that of the scribes and Pharisees." And "blessed are you when they insult you and . . . utter every kind of evil against you falsely because of me." If Christians refuse to "take a false oath," they can expect to be vilified by the world that remains utterly threatened by those who live lives of uncompromising integrity without a shred of derision or treachery.

Seventh Sunday in Ordinary Time

The Pattern of the Passion
Matthew 5:38-48

Everything that Jesus tells us to do in today's Gospel he undertakes or experiences himself in his Passion. The program for moral righteousness that Christ outlines anticipates the sacrificial self-giving of the crucifixion.

In order to fulfill the Father's will, Jesus offers no resistance to the evildoers who perpetrate his Passion. The Lord does not turn away from those who strike, not only his face, but his entire body (Mt 26:67-68). This is not to debunk justice, but rather to usher in the justice of heaven. At the end of the world, angels will separate the good from the evil (Mt 13:49) according to each one's obedience to the demands of the Kingdom.

The instance of others suing us for our tunic is reduced due to Christ's instruction to his disciples not to carry an extra one (Mt 10:10). Yet, upon demand we are to hand over our cloak, even as Jesus hands over his own life. Jesus' own cloak will be handed over to those who crucify him (Mt 27:35). But who knows? Perhaps our handed-over cloak will be like one of those privileged to be spread on the road to welcome a triumphant Jesus (Mt 21:7-8). Only such detachment predisposes us for Paschal transfiguration (Mt 17:2).

As onerous as it seems to us, we must comply generously with those who press us into service, just as Simon the Cyrenian is pressed into service in carrying the cross of Christ (Mt 27:32). For to submit to such labor unites us more closely to the cross and to our Redeemer.

Similarly, to the borrower (Mt 18:27) we must show no reluctance in giving. What we have received through Christ is a gift we must in turn give (Mt 10:8). Such liberality must never flag, even when we think we have nothing sufficient to give (Mt 14:16). In fact, Gospel giving is the fruit of renouncing all self-reliance (Mt 19:21). To those devoted to Gospel self-donation, Christ will provide even miraculous means of giving (Mt 17:27). In Jesus Christ, we discover the rationale for prudent giving

(Mt 22:21). On his return at the Second Coming, in the administration of the justice of heaven, Christ will judge us according to the fidelity of our giving (Mt 25:35-46). Furthermore, those who are accustomed to such charitable giving will be well prepared to administer the very authority given to the risen Jesus (Mt 28:18).

Likewise, worldly logic cannot reveal the Gospel way of dealing with enemies, who can be found even in our own household (Mt 10:36) and in our spiritual life (Mt 13:24-30, 36-43). In God's time, our enemies will be put beneath our feet (Mt 22:44). But in the meantime, we must pray for our persecutors, even as Christ does on the cross. For our persecutors are those most in need of God's mercy since they are so quick to abandon God's Word (Mt 13:21). Persecution proffers us the occasion to grow in holiness (Mt 5:10-12). And, as interminable as it may seem, persecution will come to an end through the coming of Jesus Christ (Mt 10:23).

Such allegiance to the justice of heaven blesses us with a recompense that far surpasses that enjoyed by tax collectors and pagans. Suffering for God's sake (Mt 5:12), spiritual hiddenness (Mt 6:1-2, 5, 16), and the unconditional welcoming of Christ and his teaching (Mt 10:41-42) grace us with a prophet's reward — a reward that cannot be gained apart from the cross of Jesus Christ.

The heavenly Father is perfect because of the perfect way he generates us with his merciful, provident, paternal care. Our perfection consists in embracing the Father's will as humble, devoted, and confident children — even if it means taking up the cross. And it does.

EIGHTH SUNDAY IN ORDINARY TIME

PIETY VS. PAGANISM
Matthew 6:24-34

The night before he dies, Jesus says to his disciples, "I no longer call you slaves. . . . I have called you friends" (Jn 15:15). Starting with today's passage, the Gospel of Matthew presents the process of progressive transformation from servant to friend. The sine qua non of servitude is steadfast devotion to a single master. Thus, the fundamental choice in the Christian life concerns serving either God or mammon.

However, the image of the master, Christ's symbol for God, differs radically from that of the stereotypical slave-owner. For the divine Master compassionately consoles his servants when they become agitated by the Enemy (Mt 13:27). Moreover, the Master is filled with an exorbitant pity that prompts him to cancel the servant's debts toward him (Mt 18:27). The Master goes out himself tirelessly to hire workers for his vineyard whom he pays beyond their merits (Mt 20:1-16). Even more, the Master has no qualms about putting reliable servants in charge of his household (Mt 24:45-47). And the Master eagerly promotes and elevates the servant, calling him to share in his joy like a son (Mt 25:20-23).

Yet, when faced with so many pressures and threats in life that cause us to obsess over our security, well-being, and success, it is easy to lose sight of this good Master who deserves all our love and obeisance. Trepidation over life's incidentals blinds us to the beauty of the Master who must — for the sake of our perfection — be served with a pure and undivided heart. Conversely, self-serving leads us to despise God and our childlike littleness (Mt 18:10).

To serve the Master means refusing to give in to the idolatry of worry over personal effects, even when faced by persecution (Mt 10:19) and the allure of the world (Mt 13:22). Just as Providence supplies for birds (Mt 8:20; 13:32), so will God provide for the soul who lives in devotion and obedience to the Master. In our hunger, thirst, estrangement, nakedness, illness, and imprisonment, God relies on those who seek the kingdom of God and its righteousness to be the instruments to provide for us (Mt 25:31-40). In the Eucharist, the Lord blesses us with food that far surpasses whatever might be gathered. The glory of Christ's transfiguration vests us with a splendor excelling that of nature and fashion.

Thus, to serve the Lord means divesting ourselves of all the fruitless anxiety that keeps us in a state of "little faith." Christ commands us to seek first the righteousness of the Kingdom precisely by hungering and thirsting after holiness (Mt 5:6) and by welcoming persecution for holiness' sake (Mt 5:10). Without such selfless, single-hearted devotion, our righteousness remains no better than that of the scribes and Pharisees (Mt 5:20).

In short, today's Gospel challenges us to choose between piety and paganism. The pagans are those who do not reach out to strangers (Mt 5:47), who pray in multiplied rattling (Mt 6:7), who persecute Christians (Mt 10:18; 20:19), who refuse to repent of sin (Mt 18:17), and who lord their authority over others (Mt 20:25). However, the pious servant is the one who, through grace-filled obedience, becomes like his Master (Mt 10:25). He does this by allowing the weeds to grow along with the wheat in his soul until harvest (Mt 13:24-30); by fulfilling the mission of the Master, even when it means persecution (Mt 21:33-44); by summoning others to the Master's wedding feast (Mt 22:1-10); by remaining vigilant and diligent (Mt 24:45-50); by making the most of the supernatural investment the Master hands over to him (Mt 25:14-30); and by serving the needs of all (Mt 20:27). Such heartfelt devotion keeps us always mindful of the goodness of the Master and committed to the truth that makes us God's friends.

Ninth Sunday in Ordinary Time

Known by Jesus
Matthew 7:21-27

Can we imagine anything more horrifying than for Jesus Christ to claim that he never knew us? Yet, the Lord maintains that he will solemnly make this very declaration to those who appeal to him without first abandoning themselves to the will of the Father (Mt 10:32-33). There is no merit in our prophesying, driving out demons, or doing other mighty deeds if those accomplishments defy the will of the Father. For it is not the illustriousness of our actions that gains us access to heaven, but rather our intimate union with the Father as children completely devoted to his will. The disciple who wants to bury his father (Mt 8:21) and the hardhearted "goats" of the Last Judgment (Mt 25:44) stand as examples of those who cry out "Lord, Lord" without conforming themselves to the Father's will.

Thus, we must abdicate all misconceived notions of discipleship, and assimilate and appropriate the will of the Father. Jesus forms us for the Father's will from the first moments of his teaching. Christ instructs us to pray that the Father's will be done (Mt 6:10). Jesus reveals that mercy toward sinners is the heart of the Father's will (Mt 9:13; 12:7). Doing the will of the Father incorporates us into the family of God (Mt 12:50). The Father's will remains particularly concerned with the littlest ones who get lost (Mt 18:14). And the will of the Father fortifies us for our greatest agonies (Mt 26:42).

In other words, to do the will of the Father entails prayerful renunciation of self-will, generous compassion and forgiveness toward others, the willingness to receive a new identity in God, solicitude toward the poor and the needy, and unmitigated self-donation in the face of suffering. If we do not disown our presumptuous assumptions about what qualifies us for heaven, then we ourselves will be disowned.

Thus, to get into heaven we must be known by the Lord, and to be known by the Lord we must know the Lord. We come to know the Lord by listening and acting on his words that reveal the will of the Father.

51

The Father himself adjures us to listen (Mt 17:5), for the everlasting words of Jesus (Mt 24:35) possess a power that is effective and healing even from a great distance (Mt 8:8, 16). Faithful adherence to the Gospel becomes a kind of house where we dwell, where we remain protected from the assaulting elements, and where we are blessed with security. The Word of God takes the buffeting winds to task (Mt 8:26-27) and enables the faithful disciple to walk upon the floods (Mt 14:22-33).

One's allegiance to the will of the Father through dedication to Christ's words distinguishes the "wise man" (Mt 10:16; 24:45; 25:2-9) from the "fool" (Mt 5:22; 23:17; 25:2-8). To live without a home is to live in peril, yet the strength of any house depends on the firmness of its foundation. To build outside of Jesus' word and the Father's will is to become completely ruined — literally "fallen." Christ's declaration to those who reject the will of the Father imitates the sentence of the master to the worthless third servant of the parable (Mt 25:30). In both cases, the evildoers bring their demise upon themselves through their own self-absorption and infidelity. They are not caught up into the home of heaven because they are so caught up in themselves.

However, to build our house on the rock of Peter (Mt 16:18) — that is, the Church — assures us of an abode that prefigures our ultimate dwelling, and that predisposes us for our ultimate communion with God in the kingdom of heaven. The Lord knows us through our union with the Church.

First Sunday of Lent

The Temptations and the Lord's Prayer
Matthew 4:1-11

What was Jesus' course of defense when confronted with the temptations in the desert? Perhaps it was in this wasteland that, for the first time, Jesus prayed, "Lead us not into temptation." Even more, perhaps the experience of the temptations was the catalyst for Christ to compose the Lord's Prayer.

Notice how the tempter begins each temptation with the words "If you are the Son of God," indicating that the temptations deliberately call into question the veracity of Christ's status as God's Son. Satan's diabolical treachery aims to deceive Jesus into disowning his divine Sonship and disavowing his relationship with his Father. Marvelously, Christ's deftness in dealing with the temptations effects the very opposite response: it confirms beyond question his identity as Son, and it intensifies his absolute allegiance to the will of his Father through his own total gift of self. In short, the temptations provide a deeply human experience that shows Jesus how to teach us how to know, love, and worship the Father.

After his forty days of fasting, Christ is confronted by the inescapable anguish of hunger. The natural instinct for survival tells Jesus that it is fitting for him to seek the food necessary to sustain life, and the devious devil capitalizes on this impulse: if Jesus is God's Son, of course his Father would want him to stay alive at any cost. But the agony of hunger convinces Christ that there is a greater good than life — namely, the love of the Father. To be perfect as the heavenly Father is perfect means letting the Father feed us with the food he himself provides. We abandon ourselves in confidence and devotion to the paternal care of the Father every time we pray, "Give us this day our daily bread."

Perhaps it was owing to his scrape with hunger in the desert that Jesus decided to remain ever-present to us in the food of the Eucharist. For Christ himself knows how much the conflict caused by hunger can lead the committed soul to that self-emptying that claims the Father in

53

the fullness of his love and providence. That love remains the ultimate, inescapable longing of our heart.

If God is a good Father, then what could give him greater joy than demonstrating his power and protection to his children? So goes the duplicity of the devil's second temptation. The tempter's urging seems admirable for, by throwing himself off the temple, Jesus will give God the chance to prove just how powerful a Father he is. However, what tries to pass itself off as piety is in reality nothing less than blasphemous defiance that dares the Father as an ultimatum to display his guardianship. To be sure, when we are imperiled by the effects of the Fall, the only righteous way to gain the Father's support is to throw ourselves upon God's mercy. Jesus will instruct us to pray, "deliver us from evil," especially as the Evil One leads us to test the Father's benevolence. At the same time, Jesus teaches us the reciprocal dynamics of Gospel forgiveness so as to avoid all sordid and unsound ploys to gain God's aid.

If the first temptation poses a challenge to Jesus' love of his Father, and the second to the virtue of hope in the Son's relationship with the Father, the third temptation endeavors to nullify faith. The tempter believes that the mere sight of worldly magnificence will divert the Son from his mission of establishing the kingdom of God on earth. But from all eternity, the Son of God has beheld the unfathomable splendor of the Father's face. Nothing can beguile him from that glory. Yet, how readily we compromise our supreme dignity in order to indulge in the idols of the world. Christ knows that the only thing that will keep us from worshiping the father of lies is unfailing worship of the Father. For he alone is our Father.

SECOND SUNDAY OF LENT

THE GLORY OF THE BEAUTIFUL
Matthew 17:1-9

In the mind of St. Thomas Aquinas, three conditions are necessary for something to be beautiful. These conditions are preeminently present at Christ's transfiguration. First of all, for something to be beautiful there must be *integrity* – that is, the perfection and completeness of the essential parts of a thing. In the Transfiguration, this fullness of being appears in the presence of all three Persons of the Blessed Trinity, Moses and Elijah, and also Christ's three closest apostles. Moreover, the beautiful relies on *proportion* – the harmonious balancing and order of these parts. In the Transfiguration, Christ himself is the center, the voice of the Father and the Holy Spirit (the cloud) hover above Jesus, Moses and Elijah converse with Jesus, and the apostles lie prostrate below Jesus.

However, the third condition of beauty is the most celebrated one of the Transfiguration: *radiance* or *clarity*. Radiance is that special quality of brilliance that shines from the form, enabling the viewer to grasp the richness of the form's perfection. The intelligibility of radiance or clarity appeals to our reason and leads us to contemplate the resplendence of the ideal communicated. The glory of Christ's Person radiates from his body revealing his divinity, and readying us for the Resurrection by way of the Passion.

We need this experience of eternal beauty in order to become transfigured ourselves. The philosopher Jacques Maritain once wrote, "If people remain in the world of their sentimental egos, they do not understand each other. Let them touch the beautiful, then contact is made, souls communicate." The Transfiguration lifts us out of our sentimental egos and touches us to the supremely beautiful so that our souls can communicate worthily with God. In the words of St. Thomas, "It was fitting that Christ should show his disciples the glory of his radiance, to which he will configure those who are his." For Christ wished to be transfigured in order to arouse in us a desire to share in his glory.

How does the Transfiguration take place in us? St. Thomas explains,

"Beauty is found by participation in the moral virtues, inasmuch as they participate in the order of reason." He notes that this is especially so of temperance, "which represses the movements of concupiscence that are most muddling to the light of reason."

The Byzantine liturgy proclaims, "Through your Transfiguration, O Christ, you returned Adam's nature to its original splendor, restoring its very elements to the glory and brilliance of your divinity." To become transfigured means claiming the image-restoration and perfection made possible in Jesus Christ. It means recognizing that the beauty of our spiritual life demands an integrity, a proportion, and a radiance that flow uniquely from our union with the Body of Christ.

As St. Thomas suggests, the sign that Christ intends this kind of moral transfiguration for us personally appears in the radiance of his own garments, which prefigures the future splendor of the saints. Nevertheless, we must not forget that the Transfiguration on Tabor anticipates the disfiguration on Calvary. The only means to resurrection is via the Passion. Yet, the Transfiguration fortifies us to see "Jesus alone" in all the trials and struggles of the remaining days of Lent. In a poem, St. Catherine of Siena observes, "O gentle loving Word, you had to suffer in order to enter into your very self!" We, too, enter into the divine self whom Christ reveals in the Transfiguration the same way he does: through suffering.

THIRD SUNDAY OF LENT

THE PROCESS OF CONVERSION
John 4:5-42

When Jesus meets the Samaritan woman at the well, the woman has many options, including that of ignoring Christ and walking away. The fact that she entertains Jesus' question by replying with one of her own indicates an openness on her part to the efficacy of the Word of God. This predisposition is the seedbed for conversion. Her willingness to listen to the Lord indicates a degree of divine grace already at work in her, inchoately conforming her to Christ.

Jesus responds to the woman's question by proclaiming the Good News to her: "The gift of God . . . would have given you living water." Through this act of preaching, Christ exteriorly presents God's offer of salvation to the woman in response to her real human problem of thirst. The searching soul eagerly listens to such an epiphany of grace that proffers so much promise.

For us as well, the preaching of the Gospel effects a saving encounter with Jesus Christ, in which the process of justification begins to take hold of our life. The Word we hear inaugurates the salvific initiative that detaches us from sin, effects in us that rectitude of divine love that is righteousness, and establishes in us a holy cooperation between God's grace and our human freedom.

Once the woman believes in her mind that Jesus is telling the truth, she begins to desire it in her heart: "Sir, give me this water." In the process of conversion, what is first apprehended and approved by the intellect is then presented to the will. Under the impetus of grace, the will in turn acts to choose the good that the Gospel promises. The woman declares, "Sir, I can see that you are a prophet." With this confession, she begins to see beyond the convenience of the water she needs to the greater good of possessing God. By using her freedom to reach out for something good precisely because it is godly, the woman takes the crucial step in renouncing the false goods and evil choices that she has made in the past.

57

The conformed desires of her heart next impact the convictions of her mind. The woman accepts Christ as the Messiah. In other words, her will has commanded her intellect to assent to the truth proposed. Animated by the Truth, the woman begins to live fully by faith. The Gospel that now enlightens her intellect and will energizes her, enabling her to embrace the Mystery with her whole being.

Trusting in this life-giving Truth, the woman leaves behind her water jar and goes off proclaiming to the town that Jesus is the Messiah. Enflamed with that confidence which is the fruit of communion with Christ, her reason is able to assent to what exceeds its natural capacities. With conviction she testifies that Christ is "truly the Savior of the world" — a reality that no natural science can "prove."

In fact, so persuasive is her testimony that "many of the Samaritans of that town began to believe in him." The woman's word is imbued with the very authority of the Word of God. The authenticity of the grace of justification that transforms the woman — and, through her agency, the town — appears in the Samaritans' invitation to Christ "to stay with them." Jesus complies and stays there for two days — a fact that reminds us that genuine holiness is realized through the process of ongoing conversion, which requires intimate contact with the Person of Christ and attentive responsiveness to the Word of his Gospel and the grace that it offers: the Gift of God.

Fourth Sunday of Lent

Seeing the I AM
John 9:1-41

At the beginning of the long passage about healing the man born blind, Jesus claims, "We have to do the works of the one who sent me." The Father's works are creation, redemption, and sanctification. In taking them on, Christ destroys the works of the devil (1 Jn 3:8), in particular the treacherous seduction that led mankind into rebellious disobedience of God.

Jesus accomplishes the works of the Father quite concretely and explicitly in today's Gospel. It is altogether possible for the Lord to heal the blind man without touching him or without the use of any substance. But Christ's act of smearing the blind man's eyes with homemade clay recalls that moment in the Book of Genesis when God forms the first man out of the clay of the earth (Gn 2:7). In other words, Christ's healing of the blind man is a kind of re-creation.

Furthermore, the blind man washes in the pool and comes back "able to see." The washing liberates him from the night of blindness "when no one can work." That is, he has been redeemed by the Light of the World — a redemption whereby he so much belongs to God that he can at last benefit from and participate in the power of divine light. The act of washing that Jesus commands is baptismal. The only other washing mentioned in the Gospel of John is one that Christ enacts himself the night before he dies when he washes his apostles' feet. Both instances point to the redemption in Christ's blood: "The blood of his Son Jesus cleanses us from all sin" (1 Jn 1:7).

John informs us that the blind man comes back "able to see," but notice that he has not yet *actually* seen Jesus Christ. Sanctification consists in "seeing" Jesus. And seeing Jesus requires interior communion with Christ, a personal relationship of love with him, and being touched by the Holy Spirit to understand the inner meaning of Christ's actions. Jesus personally takes the initiative in sanctifying the blind man by "finding him." Christ confirms that the healed man possesses the prerequi-

59

sites for sanctification by declaring, "You have seen him." The sanctified man responds by calling Jesus "Lord" and by worshiping him.

Early on, Jesus insists that this man was born blind "so that the works of God might be made visible through him." Prior to his encounter with Christ, everything was "invisible" to the blind man. After his encounter with Christ, the very works of the Father become visible in the man who can miraculously see. But how can this be, since Jesus Christ himself is the one through whom the Father and his love become visible to us (1 Jn 1:1-2; 4:9)?

The Evangelist answers this. When the neighbors ask the blind man if he is the same unsighted beggar whom they had all known, the blind man replies, "I am." The only other person who uses this expression in the Gospel of John is the Son of God himself — some twenty-seven times (Jn 4:26; 6:20, 35, 41, 48, 51; 8:12, 24, 28, 58; 9:5; 10:7, 9, 11, 14, 36; 11:25; 13:13, 19; 14:6; 15:1, 5; 18:5, 6, 8, 37; 19:21). Whenever Christ says "I AM," he identifies himself with Almighty God — "I AM WHO AM" — who reveals himself to Moses (Ex 3:14). In other words, through his re-creation, redemption, and sanctification, the blind man is presented to us as *another Christ* who manifests the saving power of God.

In short, the point of the story of the healing of the blind man is that anyone who rejects the blinding rebellion of the devil and obediently submits to Christ's re-creating, redeeming, and sanctifying power will become the Light of Christ in whom the Father's works gloriously appear. That is the true joy of this Laetare Sunday.

FIFTH SUNDAY OF LENT

TABOR AT LAZARUS' TOMB
John 11:1-45

Keep in mind that in the Gospel of John there is no account of the Transfiguration. With the first verse, John's Gospel begins its project of placing special emphasis on the divinity of the Word of God incarnate in Jesus, the Son of God. In fact, as the opening lines suggest, the Gospel of John is like one great, prolonged encounter with the Transfiguration: "We saw his glory" (Jn 1:14). St. John Chrysostom notes that the evangelist "John who enters into higher statements regarding Christ's nature than any of the other evangelists also descends lower than any in describing his bodily affections." There is a definite purpose for such stress on the humanity of Jesus in the Gospel passage today.

In Matthew, Mark, and Luke (the synoptic Gospels), the Transfiguration gloriously reveals the divinity of Christ and the depths of his obedient union with the Father, an obedience ordered to his Passion and death. One of Christ's motives in the Transfiguration is to prepare his disciples for Calvary and the Resurrection. In this way, the experience of the Transfiguration enables the disciples to believe in Jesus' Resurrection when they are confronted with the empty tomb. Ironically, the raising of Lazarus is effectively the antithesis of the Transfiguration, but one that achieves the same end. Notice how similar the outcome of the raising of Lazarus is to the Transfiguration, but in a converse way.

Whereas Christ's divinity becomes transparent at the Transfiguration in the radiance of his appearance, in this episode we are given a greater glimpse into the glory of Christ's divinity through the humbleness of his humanity. John tells us that Jesus was "perturbed," "deeply troubled," and that he "wept." As St. John Chrysostom assesses it, "That Jesus wept and groaned are mentioned to show us the reality of his human nature." Moreover, this weeping is not a sign of weakness but rather of reverent self-giving that prompts Jesus to pray aloud to the Father. The Letter to the Hebrews asserts that Jesus "offered prayers and supplications with loud cries and tears to [God] . . . and he was heard because of his reverence" (Heb 5:7). In the synoptic accounts of the Transfiguration, we hear the voice of the Father from the heavens confirming his love for his Son. However, in this account we hear instead the voice of the Son praying to the Father who always hears him. However, although in different ways, both occasions testify to Christ's total submission to his Father's will.

Unlike at the Transfiguration, those present at the raising of Lazarus are transfixed, not by the spectacular and the resplendent, but by the mundane and the moribund. The climactic focus is not on the dazzling clothes of Christ but on the death rags of Lazarus. Nevertheless, both reveal the glory of Jesus Christ. As St. John Chrysostom writes, "In condescension to those present, Christ humbled himself and let his human nature be seen in order to gain them as witnesses to the miracle."

The raising of Lazarus readies those who experience it for the Resurrection of Jesus Christ. This miracle strengthens our belief that enables us to "see the glory of God." But Jesus Christ is glorified on the cross. Thus, for John the Evangelist, our sharing in Christ's transfiguration means refusing to be put off by the stink in our life, taking away the stones that obstruct us from personal communion with Jesus, and untying anything that binds our God-ordered freedom. In short, our sharing in the Resurrection of Christ means uniting ourselves to his suffering and death. Although no one will physically witness the moment when Jesus Christ comes out of his tomb on Easter, the event continues to transfigure us because of our resolute belief in Jesus Christ, "the resurrection and the life." We truly see.

Palm Sunday of the Lord's Passion

Profession, Prayer, and Passover
Matthew 26:14-27:66

To insure that we make this week holy, we need simply to fulfill Christ's three commands in today's account of the Passion. At the moment of the betrayal in the Garden of Gethsemane, Jesus says to his apostle, "Put your sword back into its sheath." To participate worthily in the Passion of Jesus Christ means putting an end to all the aggression, anger, antagonism, resentment, and hostility that commandeers our life. Christians do not live by impulse, by violence, or by the whim of egoistic will. To do so is to betray the truth of the Gospel. Rather, we are called to live by faith.

Yet, that faith-living is what the self-absorbed Judas betrays. As the Orthodox liturgy of Holy Week laments, "What caused you to betray the Savior, O Judas? Did he expel you from the ranks of the apostles? Did he take from you the gift of healing? Did he send you from the table while taking supper with the others? Did he wash their feet and pass you by? How have you forgotten such good things? Your ingratitude is notorious, but his boundless long-suffering and great mercy are proclaimed to all."

Msgr. Luigi Giussani explains that betrayal is the exact opposite of profession. He writes, " 'Profession' means to affirm before the world, and 'betrayal' means to deny before the world." To realize the rich graces of Holy Week means living to the fullest the Profession of Faith that we make at Mass this Passion Sunday.

As much as we abhor shouting out, "Let him be crucified!" during the recitation of the Passion at Mass, the sinful actions that we have silently condoned in our life in fact sanction that death sentence. Professing faith means owning up to our responsibility in the crucifixion of Jesus Christ. For only the cross of Christ will save us from ourselves. As the Byzantine liturgy exclaims, "Come, O faithful, let us adore the life-giving cross of Christ, the King of glory, for when he extended his arms on it of his own free will, he restored us to the original bliss. Come, O faithful, let us adore the cross through which we have been made worthy to crush the devil's head."

Furthermore, in the garden Jesus commands his disciples, "Watch and pray." We must be watchful of anything that alienates us from God — not only gross and evil things but even seemingly negligible indulgences that can sneak up on us as easily and innocently as sleep. Holiness requires remaining vigilant to anything that compromises our active personal union with Jesus Christ. We rely on prayer to intensify that communion and to fortify us for moments of temptation and delusion. The slivers of palm that we carry home today to place on our crucifixes and in other sacred places encourage us to pray with ever-deeper devotion to the Passion of Jesus Christ. As we see the palms that signify Christ's victorious entrance into Jerusalem, we are reminded to remain watchful as we participate in the agony of Gethsemane.

And finally, we make this week holy by entering into the house of God to celebrate the Passover of Jesus Christ. The sacraments are the way that we remain personally united to the Passion of Jesus Christ and to the saving power of the Paschal Mystery. Fr. Antonin Sertillanges, O.P., once wrote, "The triumph of Jesus on Palm Sunday was actually a march toward Calvary, and he knew it. Thus the triumph of the Christian to baptism, confirmation, first Communion, marriage, the priesthood or religious profession, is and ought to be a march to Calvary. Happy are they who realize this, consent to it, and find in this very truth their consolation."

EASTER SUNDAY

APPROACH, EMBRACE, WORSHIP
Matthew 28:1-10

When we have grasped God with our mind and set our heart on "seeking Jesus the crucified," nothing can stand in our way. Today the two Marys in the Gospel have to contend with the darkness of early morning in the cemetery, a great earthquake, the rebuff of the guards, the apparition of an angel, and a stupefying encounter with the risen Jesus himself.

However, the greatest obstacle to union with Christ comes from within: fear. It is fear that shakes the guards and turns them into the antithesis of Easter — "dead men." The angel warns the women not to be afraid, and Jesus himself reiterates the command. His words recall his instruction to his apostles at the Transfiguration (Mt 17:6-7; the angel's white-as-snow clothing copies that of the transfigured Lord, Mt 17:2). These words that mark the Resurrection of Jesus also distinguish his conception. The angel appears to Joseph and tells him to have no fear about taking Mary as his wife (Mt 1:20). Jesus teaches that we should only fear the One who can destroy both body and soul in Gehenna (Mt 10:28). But that is the fear of the believer who recognizes the merciful God's desire, not to destroy, but to restore life by reuniting body and soul in the Resurrection of Jesus Christ. Thus, we need to come in contact with the overwhelmingly frightful in order to discover how much the overpowering grace of the Resurrection transfigures our life in mercy.

The women's triumph over the antagonist of fear appears in the form of joy. Their joy is a continuation of the joy experienced by the Magi (Mt 2:10), the persecuted (Mt 5:12), those who hear the Word (Mt 13:20), the one who finds the treasure of the Kingdom (Mt 13:44), the good shepherd upon finding the lost sheep (Mt 18:13), and the master because of his reliable servants (Mt 25:21, 23). In other words, the joy that sends the women running away from the tomb and back to the disciples is rooted in finding Jesus in the darkness, in the beatitude of maltreatment, and in faithfulness to the good news proclaimed by the angel. They are

65

overjoyed because the risen Shepherd has found them, and in him they have found the treasure of their hearts. Because of their industriousness and piety, the women can share in their Master's Paschal joy. Even before seeing the risen Jesus, the women resolve to become heralds of joy to the others.

The women approach the Lord, embrace Jesus' feet, and do him homage. Their actions reveal the pattern of faith by which all the rich graces of Easter become our own. The women approach Jesus — this means that they leave everything else behind: their plans, their regrets, their fears, their procrastination, and their excuses.

They make Jesus the chief priority in their lives by actually, concretely going to him. The women unite themselves to Jesus by embracing his feet. While on the mountain by the Sea of Galilee, large crowds brought cripples, the deformed, the blind, the mute, and many others in need to Jesus and "placed them at his feet" (Mt 15:30). Easter calls us to lay at the feet of our risen Savior all our defects, weaknesses, shortcomings, failures, and deficiencies, confident that the Redeemer will cure them.

And the women did him homage. The Resurrection blesses us with that justification whereby we can worship God in righteousness. To perpetuate the graces of Easter we must pray unceasingly and make the liturgy the source and summit of our life.

Jesus promises that in Galilee his disciples "will see me." If we cast off fear and approach the risen Jesus, embrace him, and worship him, then, like the disciples at the Transfiguration, we will see "no one else but Jesus" (Mt 17:8).

SECOND SUNDAY OF EASTER

JOHN'S SERMON ON THE MOUNT
John 20:19-31

The Gospel of John does not recount Christ's Sermon on the Mount. Instead, the closest we get to a proclamation of the Beatitudes in John comes in today's Gospel when the risen Jesus says to doubting Thomas, "Blessed are those who have not seen and have believed." The heart of the Beatitudes, which the resurrected Lord underscores today, is "blessed are the pure of heart, for they shall see God." It is precisely that purity that Thomas lacks.

The doubt of the apostle Thomas is far more common to the Christian life than we may care to admit. The *Catechism* notes that the most common temptation for believers is a lack of faith that "expresses itself less by declared incredulity than by our actual preferences" (2732). So it is with Thomas. It is not that he absolutely refuses to believe, that he finds the whole notion of resurrection preposterous. Rather, Thomas opts to suspend his belief until proof is produced that fulfills his actual preferences — "Unless I put my finger into the nailmarks. . . ."

Thomas will never truly "see" Jesus until he changes the actual, disordered preferences of his heart. The hardness, the obduracy of his heart must be purified. Only such a renunciation of willfulness and self-centeredness in favor of Gospel humility and self-abandonment can effect the requisite purity of heart whereby we become graced to see God.

For the truth is that Thomas had already been offered the opportunity to see the risen Lord — in his fellow disciples. When those who encountered Christ in that locked room on the first day of the week in turn declared to Thomas, "We have seen the Lord," they were not boasting or merely making a remarkable report. Rather, they were attesting to what had transpired in their own souls. Their announcement had none of the sensationalism of the press releases of those who claim to have seen a UFO. In fact, in their simple statement the disciples in no way *beg* others to believe. They do not need to.

Anyone with a pure heart, hearing the words — the profession of faith — of these apostles, will know and believe that *they have* seen the risen Lord in them. The effects of Easter are evident in the way the Resurrection has concretely changed their lives. That personal transformation in grace testifies to the truthfulness of the Resurrection. Easter peace is palpable.

To see such a Paschal change in others, however, requires a willingness to be so changed ourselves. It boils down to relying on Gospel "seeing" instead of insisting upon worldly "feeling." The *Catechism* warns us that we cannot "rely on our feelings or our works to conclude that we are justified and saved" (2005). In fact, "strong feelings are not decisive for the morality or the holiness of persons" (1768). Rather, "faith is a filial adherence to God beyond what we feel and understand. It is possible because the beloved Son gives us access to the Father" (2609). That access to the Father is more important and more effective for our salvation than even feeling the wounds of Jesus with our own hands.

No wonder, then, that phenomenal miracles are not the ordinary way that Christ ordains to lead others to belief. As the evangelist John declares, "These [signs] are written that you may come to believe." Belief comes through hearing, not seeing. The word-signs of the Gospel enable us to seize with our minds the truth of the Resurrection. Blessed are those who need nothing more stupendous in order to believe. What Jesus says to his disciples after washing their feet he says to us who have been saved from the doubtfulness of Thomas: "If you understand this, blessed are you if you do it" (Jn 13:17). In the witness of our transformed lives of faith, others will see the Lord.

THIRD SUNDAY OF EASTER

ABUNDANT AND BURNING OF HEART
Luke 24:13-35

Notice all the different forms of discourse featured in today's Gospel: conversing, debating, discussing, replying, prophesying, reporting, announcing, describing, interpreting, speaking, saying, recounting. In trying to describe Jesus to the unrecognized Jesus, the two disciples on the road to Emmaus identify him as "a prophet mighty in deed and word." And yet, they themselves fail to heed his word — a neglectfulness that prevents them from recognizing Christ. It prompts the Lord to say to them, "Oh, how foolish you are! How slow of heart to believe all that the prophets spoke!"

There is an ulterior warning — even an indictment — for those who are especially attentive and attuned to the clues given in this Gospel. The "conversing and debating" of the two disciples linguistically recalls the dispute at the Last Supper about the identity of Christ's betrayer (Lk 22:23). The exchange on the way to Emmaus betrays that the disciples' conviction about the identity of Christ is not sufficiently strong. Similarly, the other Gospel occasions of "discussions" (Lk 9:46; 20:5; 20:14) all concern either faithlessness or betrayal. Sometimes dialogue is less than constructive. The expression for the "downcast look" that brands the disciples when Christ questions them is used only one other time in all of the Gospels — to describe the glum appearance of the faces of hypocrites (Mt 6:16).

Clearly then, this encounter with the risen Christ on the road admonishes us about just how vigilant and obedient to the Word of God we need constantly to be (Lk 10:39). Many in the Gospel are spellbound and astonished by the mighty words of Jesus (Lk 4:22, 32, 36). For Christ's words heal as they forgive (Lk 5:23). They work wondrously even from a distance (Lk 7:7). Jesus' words will not pass away (Lk 21:33), yet their effectiveness depends on our putting that Word into practice in the present moment (Lk 6:46-47; 8:8).

The announcement made to the two disciples by "some women" of their group brings to a climax the angelic annunciation to Mary (Lk 1:35, 38) and to the shepherds (Lk 2:10, 13, 17). When angels appear to the women at the tomb, their announcement consists of a reminder about the Resurrection (Lk 24:6-8). We, too, need actively to remember the truths that form and direct our life. To that end, we must regularly rely on the witness of other Christians to keep us ever mindful of the Gospel.

The living Word of God brings our slow heart up to speed. One of the chief objectives of the Incarnation indicated by the evangelist Luke is to turn the hearts of the rebellious to the wisdom of the just (Lk 1:17). That wisdom is found in God's Word. However, Christ duly cautions us that, if we are not dedicated, the devil can come and take the Word of God from our heart (Lk 8:12). As a result, all our thoughts, words, and deeds must be rooted in the Prophet mighty in word and deed. For once we accept Christ's revelation that a person speaks "from the fullness of the heart" (Lk 6:45), then we will never dismiss anyone whose words are on fire with the goodness of the Gospel. Rather, that Gospel witness will turn our slow hearts into burning hearts.

Therefore, in order to avoid a lamentation like Christ's over Jerusalem, we must remain sensitive to the numerous Emmaus moments in our own life that call us to recognize the time of our visitation (Lk 19:44) and to capitalize on the many rich graces of Easter offered to us by the Visitor to Jerusalem.

Fourth Sunday of Easter

The Voice of the Shepherd
John 10:1-10

The Gospel makes very clear that the Good Shepherd's greatest strength is not his muscle, his intelligence, or his professionalism in shepherding but rather, quite simply, his voice. This is not a surprise because, in a very real sense, our voice is who we are. Our voice reveals our interior self and the relationships that form us and give us an identity. How adept we are at forming an impression of a person we have never seen based only on the sound of his or her voice. The voice possesses the profound power to bind us interiorly with others. In the time of crisis or isolation, we become deeply consoled merely by hearing the voice of one we love. The voice of another causes what is most precious and valued to resonate in our own soul, uniting us in love with the speaker and recommitting us to what we treasure.

The centrality of Christ's voice in the relationship of the sheep — ourselves — with the Good Shepherd first appears in the Gospel of John, in John the Baptist's description of his own relationship with Jesus. Using wedding imagery, he says that the best man waits, listening for the voice of the groom — the voice that gives him joy when he hears it (Jn 3:29). Moreover, Jesus promises that those who are faithful to hearing and heeding the voice of God's Son will hear it again after their death and that it will raise them to new life (Jn 5:25, 28). However, the efficacy of the voice of Jesus Christ eludes anyone who refuses to be committed to the truth it conveys (Jn 18:37). The voice of the Father that we hear in the Gospel of John (12:28, 30; see also Jn 5:37) resounds for our sake in order to deepen our belief in and our obedience to the One he has sent.

The Good Shepherd uses his voice to do three things.

First of all, his voice calls us by name and leads us out into fertile pastures (see also Jn 1:42 and 19:4, 13 for other examples of "leading"). At climactic moments in the Gospel of John, we hear Jesus calling those close to him by name: Peter, who receives his name from Jesus (Jn 1:42); Lazarus, as Christ raises him from the dead (Jn 11:43; 12:17); and Mary

Magdalene, at the tomb, to pacify her panic over the missing body of Jesus (Jn 20:16). A name expresses one's essence, one's identity, and the meaning of one's life. Whenever we are called by name, we feel known by the other, and we are drawn into greater intimacy with the other. Christ uses his voice unceasingly to call us by name in order to assure us that we belong to him. As he calls us by name, we find our strength in his name.

Second, the "thief" (used only one other time – in reference to Judas, Jn 12:6) and the robber (Jn 18:40) differ from the Good Shepherd precisely in their attempt *not* to use their voice. Their objective "to steal and slaughter and destroy" is predicated on maintaining a perfect silence whereby they can sneak up on unsuspecting sheep, climb over the gate, and enact their evil. They know that the sheep, failing to recognize their unfamiliar voices, will only run away in fear. The voice of Jesus keeps us from their treachery by enabling us to follow only the Good Shepherd (Jn 1:43; 8:12; 12:26; 21:19, 22). We continue to follow the Good Shepherd's voice through Peter, the Chief Shepherd of the Church (Jn 21:16).

And the voice of the Good Shepherd gives us life with the abundance of the multiplied loaves (Jn 6:12-13). For the life that Jesus proffers is eternal life that flows from faith (Jn 3:15-16; 5:24, 40; 6:40, 47, 54; 11:25-26). If we desire superabundant life, then we must possess unshakeable faith. And that faith comes to us by our responding to the voice of Jesus as it remains perpetually active in the written words of the Gospel (Jn 20:31).

Fifth Sunday of Easter

Having Faith in Jesus
John 14:1-12

Faith calls us to commit our entire self to God. The *Catechism* tells us that faith is "a filial adherence to God beyond what we feel and understand" (2609). Yet, Jesus knows how much we are swayed and side-tracked by our feelings. That is why he consoles us with his counsel, "Do not let your hearts be troubled." In this regard, Christ is speaking from experience. At the death of Lazarus, Jesus was troubled in spirit (Jn 11:33). As Jesus approached his hour, he confessed, "I am troubled now" (Jn 12:27). Before announcing that there was a betrayer in their midst, Jesus "was deeply troubled" (Jn 13:21). If we live by faith, Christ assures us that our hearts will rejoice (Jn 16:22).

The reward of such firm trust in God is threefold: a heavenly dwelling place, communion with Jesus Christ, and the power to do works greater than Jesus'. From the first moments of his ministry, Christ has been preparing a place for us in his Father's house. The act of cleansing the temple (Jn 2:13-16) reveals the reverence we must have for the Father's house, for it is our final destiny. And while a slave has no permanent place in the family house, "a son always remains" (Jn 8:35). The embrace of faith effects in us that filial adherence whereby we become sons of God. By virtue of our sonship, ironically but wonderfully, the Father and Jesus will come to make their dwelling place in us (Jn 14:23).

By its nature, faith obliges us to believe in what is unseen. However, faith assures us that everything of importance is to be found in Jesus Christ. Whoever sees Jesus sees the Father. To live by faith means to see the image of God whom Jesus reveals, and to embrace that divine image as our own. To do so means giving up every misguided effort to remake ourselves according to our own image. Jesus reveals us to ourselves. Whoever sees us must see the Father reflected in us.

Christ's entire life is a revelation of the Father. The "showing" for which Philip petitions Jesus begins at the first moment of the Incarnation (Jn 1:18). However, the simple fact of being shown the good deeds of the Father does not guarantee that one will believe (Jn 10:32). No "proof" will ever be given that compels us to believe in Jesus Christ. Rather, faith arises only in those in whom dwells a predisposition of desire. The only "proof" Jesus ever shows to attest to the pricelessness of faith is the proof of his wounded hands and side (Jn 20:20). Jesus only shows his wounds to those who commit themselves to the Passion.

As a result, faith beckons us beyond the limited understanding possible to constrained human reason. Faith curbs in us all compromise and mediocrity. For Jesus is not the map, the opinion, or the career choice. Rather, Christ is the Way, the Truth, and the Life. In other words, every means, every thought and idea, every vital dynamic essential to existence on earth begins and ends in Jesus Christ. Apart from him we can do nothing, because apart from Jesus we are nothing. Adherence to Jesus ensures that where he is we too will be, even unto the ultimate communion of heaven.

Once we have sacrificed the idolatry of feelings, subordinated human understanding to the truth of the Gospel, and freely committed ourselves as children to the Father, we should not be surprised when we find ourselves doing the works of the Father in Jesus. St. John Eudes expresses it this way:

> All that is Christ's is yours: his spirit, his heart, his body and soul, and all his faculties. You must make use of all these as of your own, to serve, praise, love, and glorify God. He longs for you to use all that is in you, as if it were his own, for the service and glory of the Father.

Sixth Sunday of Easter

The Ten Commandments
John 14:15-21

One of the more pernicious recurring fads in the world is the fallacy of claiming to love Jesus Christ while at the same time eschewing the commandments and the teachings of the Church. That is like professing to love another's voice but to hate his words. It is very superficial. For the real test and testimony of our love for another lie in our devotion to what our loved one holds dear and in our obedience to the loved one's wishes. Worldly delusion wants to cloud the crucial connection between affection and duty, as if mere sentiment can suffice in the covenant between persons. The too-common occurrence of broken hearts verifies that it cannot. Lack of sentiment rarely causes heartache; neglect, disregard, and betrayal do.

"If you love me, you will keep my commandments." This is not an ultimatum but the simple statement of fact; anyone who truly loves Jesus Christ will obey the Eternal Law because of the indispensable way that it enables us to actualize our love for God. The Ten Commandments are a God-sent benefit by which we can assess what we love most in life. For the reality is that human beings *love* sin. We are loath to give up sin because we are dubious about finding anything else that gratifies us as much as we think sin does.

The Ten Commandments make it perfectly clear how much, left to ourselves, we would fall in love with idolatry, impiety, disobedience, violence, sensuality, stealing, dishonesty, and covetousness. Thus, we need the Ten Commandments in order to purify our love for Jesus. As Pope John Paul II has written, the Ten Commandments "save man from the destructive force of egoism, hatred, and falsehood. They point out all the false gods that draw him into slavery." The Ten Commandments provide the context for us to realize if we are living in ourselves or living in Christ. The Ten Commandments make us want to live God's law because they assure us there is no true life and happiness outside of it. They free us from the duplicity in which the world connives to enshroud us.

75

Moreover, when we love Jesus with the bona fide love that is formed by the Decalogue, then Christ loves us and reveals himself to us. Jesus fulfills this promise dramatically in his Resurrection appearances to his disciples (Jn 21:14). But we experience Christ's most poignant self-revelation within ourselves. Pope John Paul II notes that "to keep the commandments . . . is also to be faithful to ourselves, to our true nature and our deepest aspirations." For the Ten Commandments are "the universal moral law, valid in every time and place" that "provide the only true basis for the lives of individuals, societies, and nations." To disregard the Decalogue is to deny the very truth of ourselves. To observe the commandments is to reverence God and our divine vocation, even as Jesus does (Jn 8:55).

Finally, as Pope John Paul II makes clear, "the Ten Commandments are the law of freedom . . . [however,] it is not an impersonal law; what is required is loving surrender to the Father through Christ Jesus in the Holy Spirit." That is why Jesus promises that he will not leave us orphans. The Person of the Holy Spirit is with us always to empower us to love and to fulfill the personal law of God. The Holy Spirit comes and remains with us as once he did with John the Baptist (Jn 1:32-33) by way of the *parrhesia* — the filial trust and the certainty of being loved — that he engenders. Then, filled with the light and the realization that elude the obstinate world, we embrace the Gospel freedom that comes to us through the blessing of the Ten Commandments: "the freedom to love, to choose what is good in every situation, even when to do so is a burden."

Seventh Sunday of Easter

Glory, Belonging, and Eternal Life
John 17:1-11a

The Father glorifies his Son by giving him the cross. When the evangelist John, in speaking about the Word made flesh, attests that "we saw his glory" (Jn 1:14), he is referring specifically to Golgotha. For in Christ's crucifying act of self-sacrifice in the Passion, Jesus discloses and communicates divine goodness — the mediation that comprises the glory of God.

Reciprocally, Jesus glorifies God on the cross — Christ's accomplishment of the Father's "work." God manifests his glory by revealing and giving his holy name, and Jesus glorifies the Father by effecting this revelation. The Lord testifies, "I revealed your name to those whom you gave me." Accordingly, Jesus prays particularly for his disciples and rejoices in them because he has been glorified in them thanks to their fervent, heartfelt recognition of God as Father. The disciples come to believe in the mercy, wisdom, and providence of the Father — whom they cannot see — via the goodness and compassion of the Son made visible.

In short, God gives his glory by revealing in creation his divine holiness. We in turn glorify God by devoting ourselves to that holiness. The essence of Christian holiness entails claiming as our greatest priority the truth that we belong to God. In our regard, Jesus professes, "They belonged to you." If the glory of Jesus Christ consists in taking up the cross, accomplishing the Father's work of sanctification, and revealing God's name, then the same is true of us. Conversely, the attempt to seek glory apart from the Passion, in our own will or according to our own name, leads only to the futility and fatuousness of vainglory.

Jesus prays exclusively for us today so that we will claim as our treasure the exclusive privilege of belonging to God — the key to our glory. Msgr. Luigi Giussani has explained it this way:

> If man belonged to nothing, then he would be nothing.
> Belonging implies that an "I" that was not, now is. If there

77

were not the awareness of a belonging, then man would be faced with his own nothingness. There can be no belonging to God that is not belonging to Christ. That for which the "I" is made and for which it does everything is a Presence. The man chosen by God, the baptized, can no longer stay closed in himself, or be worried and concerned as everyone else is.

In other words, to belong to God means embracing the hope whereby we confidently confess our nothingness outside of God. To belong to God means to be convicted by the faith in which we identify our true meaning and worth only in our relationship with God through Jesus Christ. And to belong to God means to engage in a life of generous charity by which every act of our life becomes an expression of our loving, intimate union with the divine presence.

Jesus implores the Father to give him glory — the crucifying death that results in life-giving Resurrection — so that the Son may give eternal life to all who belong to him in the Father. Eternal life does not begin after we die. Rather, as the Church teaches emphatically, faith is already the beginning of eternal life. That is why Christ insists that eternal life is knowing the only true God and Jesus Christ, the One he has sent. For when we live convicted by this Gospel knowledge, then we see the concrete effects of eternal life at work in us now transforming our life. We can throw off selfishness, worry, self-preoccupation, and every other distraction and delusion that keep us closed in on ourselves. And through this maturity of grace, as the *Catechism* puts it, "the moral life blossoms into eternal life in the glory of heaven" (1709).

Pentecost Sunday

The Person Known Through Relationship
John 20:19-23

The fact that human beings need bodies, whereas angelic and divine persons do not, tells us that there is something more essential to personhood than corporeality. What defines a "person" is relationship. The first thing we were ever called — son, daughter, child — signifies a relationship. The way we truly know ourselves and the way we reveal ourselves to the world is through the relationships that form our lives. To be "personal" with another is to forge a relationship.

Since the Holy Spirit has no body, often he has nobody to love him. Thus, if we want to know the divine Person of the Holy Spirit on Pentecost, we must enter into the relationship that Pentecost makes possible.

First of all, we must embrace a resolute relationship with the Truth. The Spirit of truth comes to us to guide us to all truth. Thus, all the troubling truths of our past, all the truths about our sinfulness in the present, and all the falsehoods that masquerade as truth — perverting our perception of the future — must be surrendered to the Spirit of truth to be reconciled. The failure to weed out the lies in our life can stifle the Spirit. However, faith-filled abandonment to the truth attested to by the Holy Spirit transforms us. St. Cyril of Alexandria wrote: "The Holy Spirit changes those in whom he comes to dwell and alters the whole pattern of their lives. With the Spirit within them it is quite natural for people who had been absorbed by the things of this world to become entirely other-worldly in outlook, and for cowards to become men of great courage."

Furthermore, we love the Person of the Holy Spirit by espousing the way that he empowers us to relate to those who injure and offend us: through forgiveness. The prayer over the gifts of Saturday of the Seventh Week of Easter asserts that "the Holy Spirit . . . is our forgiveness." As Fr. Colman O'Neill wrote, "It is because Christ sends the Spirit that those who thereby belong to him are able to share in his moral rectitude, to offer his sacrifice because they offer themselves, to make true satisfaction because they offer themselves, to make true satisfaction by over-coming sin in themselves and in society." The presence of the Holy Spirit in our soul fortifies us never to surrender our peace — our harmony of soul, our recollection, our rectitude, our inner strength, our dedication to grace — to beguiling emotions, vices, the onslaught of the world's hostility, deception, and so on. Instead, through our modus operandi of forgiveness, the Holy Spirit makes Jesus Christ concrete and visible.

Finally, to love the Person of the Holy Spirit means living according to the Spirit, and not according to the flesh. One preeminent place to "see" the Holy Spirit is in faith-filled disabled persons. The Holy Spirit radiates in those who seize his strength while refusing to be defeated by the defects of the body. Similarly, the Holy Spirit shines in martyrs so caught up in love with the Spirit that they are willing even to sacrifice their bodies in death.

In this way, the mystery of Pentecost is much like the experience of the maturation of a deep friendship. A precious moment arises in one's relationship with a friend when the love that binds the two turns into an unbreakable trust. The moment may be indiscernible, but the confidence and dependence shared between the two is certain and indissoluble. Through the mutual gift of self, two persons in many respects become as one. The friend discovers the truth about himself in the other. Such friend-ship unites two souls in a profound and lasting communion. Similarly, Pentecost is the moment when God perfects his friendship with his people through the Person of the Holy Spirit.

THE MOST HOLY TRINITY

TRUTH, GOODNESS, AND BEAUTY
John 3:16-18

It never occurred to the pagan mind-set to think of God as a loving Father eager to manifest his paternal love through the compassionate bestowal of mercy. And it never would have occurred to the world if the Father had not sent his Son to us in love. If Jesus had come to us merely as a messenger or as another prophet – or, even worse, as a servant – we might have some sense of the First Person of the Blessed Trinity, but we would never believe that God is a tender, loving Father. The only way we arrive at belief in that supreme mystery is through the Sonship of Jesus Christ.

It is wrong and exceedingly harmful to conceive of the First Person of the Trinity as the "Creator." In point of fact, all the Persons of the Blessed Trinity participate in the divine act of creation. Furthermore, to entertain such a grave error denies and defies the very identity of the First Person of the Godhead. God the Father's *name* is "Father" – not "Creator." Fr. Antonin Sertillanges, O.P., has written that "God is our Creator without us. He cannot be our Father without us." Therefore, in order to accept the divine revelation that the First Person of the Blessed Trinity is the Father, we must love him as such. Which means that we must love him as sons and daughters united in the Son whom he has sent. To make our own that truth about the Father remains a crucial aspect of our personal glory in God's sight.

How do we remain united to the Son? Jesus insists that belief is needed in order to have eternal life – specifically, belief that the Father "gave his only Son." The Greek verb meaning "to give" is used in the Gospel of John to signify the handing over of Jesus to his death. Therefore, to believe in the name of the only Son of God means to believe that Jesus was born to die on the cross. To believe in Jesus means possessing the conviction that the suffering of Christ is supremely good because it is the means by which "the world might be saved." Eternal life consists in knowing the Father and Jesus Christ whom he has sent (Jn 17:3).

Thus, we cannot enjoy eternal life without embracing the goodness of the cross, especially as it imposes itself on our earthly life. To the extent that we recognize the redemptive power of suffering and accept that suffering as something good in God's plan, we enter into "eternal life" even now.

Believing in the glorification of Jesus on the cross opens us to the overflowing force of the Holy Spirit from within (Jn 7:38-39). When we see the goodness of the Passion through the eyes of the Father, we manifest our readiness to be instructed by the Holy Spirit (Jn 14:26). The Holy Spirit bears witness to what it means to live the Gospel (Jn 15:26). The Holy Spirit guides us to all truth (Jn 16:13) and confirms the goodness of the Paschal Mystery. And when Truth and Goodness become united in Love, ineffable Beauty appears.

Fr. Pierre-Marie Emonet, O.P., writes that "the person conquers itself by the search for interior unity at the heart of multiplicity, of necessity at the heart of contingency of situations, of fidelity to itself at the heart of change." Accordingly, the truth of the Father unifies our hearts; the Son reveals the necessity of the cross to gain access to the source of all goodness; and the constancy of the Holy Spirit imbues our life with the beauty of unfading fidelity. Our person is "conquered" by the Three Persons of the Blessed Trinity, whose image we bear. For to share in the truth, goodness, and beauty of the Trinity is the glory for which we have been created.

The Most Holy Body and Blood of Christ

Presence, Person, Power
John 6:51-58

Hundreds of years ago, St. Thomas Aquinas posed a question that continues to fascinate us today: Why did Jesus give us his Body? If the Lord wanted to leave us a memorial of himself, why didn't he give us his miraculous powers instead — like the ability to cure the sick, calm storms, multiply food, expel demons, and raise people from the dead? And the answer is that then we would think about Jesus only as often as we think about our auto mechanic — that is, only when our car breaks down. And since Christ's supernatural powers in us would be unfailing, we would most likely never give a thought to the Source of that divine strength.

Thus, we need Christ's Body in order to be mindful of and intimately united to him. Jesus does not want us to share simply his abilities, his effects. Rather, Jesus wants us to share in his very *self*. That is why he gives us his Body. The human flesh of Jesus continues to link us and the people of every age with the timeless sacrifice of Christ on the cross. It fills us with an enduring sense of connectedness with him and with one another. The gift of Corpus Christi makes Holy Communion with the self of Jesus Christ possible in three ways.

First of all, Jesus promises that whoever eats his flesh and drinks his blood "remains in me and I in him." How much we rely on the bodily presence of loved ones to save us from the agony of loneliness and isolation. One of the worst punishments imaginable is that of depriving someone of the physical presence of other persons: solitary confinement. The void of *physical* absence quickly degenerates into the many forms of *psychological* absence that we suffer: fear, self-doubt, depression, resentment, anger, antagonism, and so on. The bodily absence of other people in our life can even drive us insane. However, the Real Presence in the Body and Blood of Jesus Christ overcomes the "real absence" that besieges our life.

We were created for the "Remaining Presence" that we experience uniquely through Holy Communion. "That for which the 'I' is made and for which it does everything is a Presence," Msgr. Luigi Giussani writes. "The person chosen by God can no longer stay closed in [on] himself, or be worried and concerned as everyone else is. It is for a Presence, the presence of Christ in his Church, that he lives and does everything."

Second, everything that we know comes through our bodily senses. The body is the gateway to all knowledge. Jesus continues that dynamic in the Eucharist. He saves us according to the distinctiveness of our human condition. For, without the Body of Christ, we might be tempted to reduce Jesus to some abstract, impersonal concept, notion, or idea, as many people unfortunately do. In the Eucharist, Jesus wants us to know his divine Person.

The philosopher Ludwig Wittgenstein once said that "the human body is the best picture of the human soul." But the Body of Christ reveals to us something even more than the human soul of Jesus. As the *Catechism* states, "the individual characteristics of Christ's body express the divine person of God's Son" (477). Through the Body of Christ, we know God and our redemption. When we eat the "true food" of the Holy Eucharist, the Lord changes the way we know: the Eucharistic Lord changes our life view, he helps us to grow up in faith, he transforms our ideas about beauty and worth, and he makes us deeply happy.

And finally, the bread come down from heaven imparts to us "eternal life"; right now we begin to "live forever" through divinization. The sign that we do have Christ's life within us is that we assume the attributes of heaven. By partaking of the Eucharist, we partake of the divine nature. The God whom we receive in the Blessed Sacrament makes us godly.

Tenth Sunday in Ordinary Time

Seeing and Hearing
Matthew 9:9-13

In the two other places where the Gospel of Matthew mentions Jesus "passing on" (Mt 9:27; 20:30), the act results in blind men receiving their sight. There seems to be an implicit parallel between Christ's giving of vision to the blind and Christ's giving of vocation to Matthew today. Like the two blind men by the roadside (Mt 20:30), Matthew is "sitting" when Jesus passes by. In both episodes, the encounter with Christ results in their "following" him (Mt 20:34). Just as the two blind men can see something supernatural in Jesus, despite the privation of physical eyesight, the Lord looks beyond mere appearances and can see a divine vocation in one currently enmeshed in the wiles of the world. The two blind men shout out to Jesus in order to secure his pity, and Jesus speaks in command to Matthew in order to transform him with his mercy.

The confirmation of the depth of this transformation is the fact that Matthew takes Jesus into his own house for a meal. The occasions of being "at table" in the Gospel of Matthew are all times of conflict. It is at table, in the presence of his guests, that Herod capitulates to the pressure to behead John the Baptist (Mt 14:9). When at table with his newfound guests, the king of the parable throws out into the night the presumptuous diner who comes improperly dressed (Mt 22:11-13). At table, the disciples criticize the loving solicitude of the anointing woman (Mt 26:7-9), thereby missing the whole point. And at table with the Twelve, Jesus announces his betrayer (Mt 26:21). Today's instance at table is no exception. When the Pharisees "see" the dining tax collectors, they perceive, not an assemblage of potential saints, but only so many "sinners."

Although the Pharisees fail to see the occasion of grace offered by Christ at table, Jesus does not fail to hear what the grumblers say to the Lord's disciples. The "hearing" of Jesus moves him to take up his ministry in Capernaum (Mt 4:12-13), to heal the centurion's servant (Mt 8:10), to withdraw to the place where he multiplies loaves and fish (Mt 14:13), and to keep silent when confronted with the treachery of Pilate (Mt 27:13-

14). In other words, the hearing of Jesus is ordered to Gospel preaching, healing, feeding, and obedience to the Father. Just as Jesus can see what lies hidden to the eye, so does he hear what we are too cowardly to say to him directly. Yet, Christ's hearing will convert us if only we will listen.

Jesus Christ desires "mercy" — the mercy at the heart of the Beatitudes (Mt 5:7) — that the two pairs of blind men beg for (Mt 9:27; 20:30-31). Jesus addresses the Pharisees now to remedy their spiritual blindness. Soon again Jesus will have to remind the hard-hearted Pharisees that it is mercy, not sacrifice, that God desires (Mt 12:7). The Canaanite woman (Mt 15:22) and the father of the possessed boy (Mt 17:15) both recognize this in Jesus and implore him for it. But one senses that the merciless Pharisees will end up like the ingrate of the parable (Mt 18:33). Indeed, before very long Jesus will denounce the Pharisees, saying, "Woe to you, you frauds! You neglect justice and mercy and good faith" (cf. Mt 23:23).

The way to avoid the blindness of the Pharisees is to "learn" (Mt 11:29; 24:32) to cherish the Gospel above everything else, as Matthew does. When we see ourselves to be like those who are "sick" (Mt 4:24; 8:16; 14:35; 17:15), then we in turn see and rejoice in Jesus as the Divine Physician who is eager to heal us (Mt 8:8, 13; 13:15; 15:28). Only then can we and will we see ourselves as truly righteous. For then all the former hypocrisy and evil that filled us within will be purified, and we will present to view a holy exterior that truly reflects the gracefulness of our soul (Mt 23:28).

Eleventh Sunday in Ordinary Time

Abandonment and Apostleship
Matthew 9:36-10:8

When Jesus sees the crowds, his heart is moved with pity because they are troubled and "abandoned." The Greek word for *abandoned* literally means "thrown down," and it is used only two other times in the Gospel of Matthew: when the crowds lay down the sick at the feet of Jesus to be cured (Mt 15:30) and when Judas throws down into the temple the silver pieces he was paid to betray Jesus (Mt 27:5). In other words, to feel "abandoned" means to be overwhelmed by a sense of helplessness and hopelessness – serious predicaments that only the compassion of Jesus Christ can transform.

However, one might wonder why the crowds were troubled and abandoned, for Jesus Christ himself was with them. Their situation helps us to understand how easy it is for us to overlook the presence of Jesus in our midst – how easy it is to get wrapped up in ourselves and absorbed in petty concerns. Jesus rescues the crowd from their helplessness and hopelessness by giving them something that will keep them from ever forgetting just how present Jesus always is in their midst. Christ blesses them with a gift that assures God's people how active, able, and involved he is vis-à-vis their lives: he gives them the apostles.

What is the rationale behind this approach? That is, why does Jesus tend to the crowd's feeling of abandonment in this way instead of by miraculously going himself to every hurting heart? And the answer is that, as the people encounter the apostles in their ministry, they encounter the transforming power of Jesus Christ. The people were well familiar with these twelve men that Jesus commissions today: they were the community's fishermen, politicians, workers, and even traitors. These twelve men also experienced the helplessness of being abandoned. And, at the Passion of Jesus, they experienced the hopelessness of being sheep without a shepherd. Jesus sends his people the apostles because we see ourselves in the weakness of the apostles. That association and empathy consoles us.

87

But we also experience the saving power of Jesus in the apostles. Through the ordained instrumentality of these men, Jesus himself *does* go personally to every hurting human heart to heal it. Every time we recite the Creed, we say, "We believe in one holy catholic and *apostolic* Church." The apostles are at the heart of our faith, the heart of our belief, the heart of the Church. The Church is apostolic because it continues to be taught, sanctified, and guided by the apostles.

Would the world have listened if the apostles had done nothing more than make the proclamation, "The kingdom of heaven is at hand!"? We weak people demand proof, and Jesus demonstrates his penetrating grasp of human nature when he commands his apostles to accompany their preaching with saving actions: curing the sick, raising the dead, cleansing lepers, and driving out demons. That is, Christ commissions his apostles to manifest their God-given mastery over the prime causes of trouble and dejection in life: illness, death, rejection, and the devil. Jesus Christ is at the center of all this relief. And the people recognize this because they clearly see and experience that Jesus Christ is the center of the apostles' lives.

In a special way, Christ's order to cleanse lepers must have shocked people and apostles alike. For it was against the law for lepers to come in contact with "clean" people. The confidence and fearlessness with which the apostles carried out this command surely convinced others of the authenticity of the Gospel. The revolution that began in this physical contact between apostles and lepers gets elevated to its most perfect incarnation when Jesus teaches his apostles to say at the Eucharist, "This is my body."

TWELFTH SUNDAY IN ORDINARY TIME

OVERCOMING FEAR
Matthew 10:26-33

Isn't it a waste of time to tell someone not to worry, not to be afraid? Putting the added burden of that demand on someone can actually make matters worse. Yet that is exactly what Jesus does today when he says, "Fear no one." Why? Because Jesus is not delivering an ultimatum. Rather, he is giving us the power to overcome crippling fear in our life.

Jesus' mandate "Do not be afraid" is not a mere admonition (otherwise we would only become more afraid!). The wicked third servant of the parable blames his dereliction regarding the talents on "fear" (Mt 25:24-30). But the wise master sees through this deceitful rationalization to the very pride and indolence that infest the "worthless" servant's soul. In other words, with the proclamation of the Gospel, fear is no longer a valid excuse for nonperformance regarding the matters of the Kingdom because the Master himself has told us not to be afraid. Christ's words, if we heed them, drive fear from our life. The Lord's pronouncement is efficacious, freeing us from the tyranny of fear and endowing us with the capacity to preserve in our souls Christ's liberating peace.

Moreover, we can be heartened that Christ's injunction not to be afraid amounts to far more than cheap advice or badgering, since for every mention of "fear" in this Gospel there is mention made of the "Father." The antidote to earthly fear consists in communion with the heavenly Father.

Jesus deflates three fears in this Gospel. The first is the fear of our secret self. We all have secrets, past sins, and things we are ashamed of that we do not want others to know about. And they can terrorize us, disable us, blackmail us. Yet, no matter how hard we conspire to conceal these things, "all will be revealed" in purgatory. Jesus gives us the grace today to confront the painful truth about ourselves so that we can live now in his glorious Truth.

What Jesus says in the darkness we are to speak in the light. But what exactly does Jesus say to us in the darkness? In the darkness of

Good Friday, Christ cries out, "My God, my God, why have you forsaken me?" (Mt 27:46). Jesus utters this cry out of mercy — not misery — in order to assure us that the only thing to fear is the state of being separated from the Father. Thus, when we speak the Father's mercy, we dispel the darkness that terrifies.

Jesus also outmaneuvers the fear of pain and death. Sometimes we let anxiety about our inability to deal with sickness, disaster, and death impair our relationship with God. However, not a single sparrow falls to the ground without the Father's knowledge. And sometimes the Father permits "falls" for our good. For what also falls to the ground with the Father's knowledge? Jesus himself: both in Gethsemane in prayer and on the road to Calvary. In delivering us from fear, Jesus wants to convince us that the Father knows and provides for the most minute matters of our life. His all-seeing providence gives us the power to deal with details over which we remain otherwise powerless.

And finally, Jesus debunks those fears related to self-worth. The world wants constantly to dupe us into believing that we are worthless. The only way out is to acknowledge the Father in prayer, because in so doing we discover ourselves. To acknowledge the Father means to acknowledge his mercy, compassion, and forgiveness. At the same time, we must be careful not to deny Jesus, especially through complaining, jealousy, worry, sensuality, neglecting prayer, or by living in an agitated, unrecollected way. We do not deny Jesus only by renouncing our religion; we deny him by the inauthenticity of our acts. But to acknowledge Jesus is to become infallibly fearless. Intrepidly we spurn trepidation.

Thirteenth Sunday in Ordinary Time

Apostolic Church
Matthew 10:37-42

In the Creed, we profess that we believe in "one holy catholic and apostolic Church." By "apostolic," we mean that the Church is founded on the apostles, Christ's chosen witnesses. The Church keeps and hands on the teaching she has heard from the apostles, and the Church continues to be taught, sanctified, and guided by the apostles, through their successors, the bishops, until Christ's return. The instruction that Jesus gives in today's Gospel is directed to the apostles as one key moment in laying the foundation of the Church.

Obviously, to be the chosen witnesses and preeminent emissaries of Jesus Christ involves a radical change of life for these men. Jesus prepares and disposes the Twelve for their apostolic vocation today. In the first part of today's Gospel, Jesus asserts how absolutely the Twelve must be conformed to the Blessed Trinity. The apostles are to love no human being more than they love Jesus, for only then will their love be fully fixed on the Father. We balk at this teaching for fear of seeming disingenuous or disloyal. But as the *Catechism* clearly teaches, "Family ties are important but not absolute" (2232). Only the love of the Father revealed in Jesus Christ is absolute. To be apostolic is to be absolute in our communion with the Father. That love forms and perfects all human relationships.

Moreover, apostleship demands the taking up of one's cross and following after Jesus. There can be no true conformity to Jesus Christ apart from union to his cross in faith. The Passion of Jesus is the very form, the internal organizing principle, of the apostle's life. The Passion alone gives meaning to the life of the Church. Of course, to take up the cross requires tremendous self-renunciation, untold sacrifice, and unspeakable suffering. Plenty find what they consider sufficient warrant to decline conformity to Christ in the deterrent of fear. In fact, the wicked third servant of the parable slyly blames fear for his inactivity because he believes it will legitimize his indolence and insolence toward the master

91

(Mt 25:25). But in refusing the challenge that the Father hands over to us via the cross, we render ourselves "worthless" (Mt 25:25; 22:8). To be apostolic is to live by faith, which entails realizing our worth exclusively in the crucifixion of Jesus.

Furthermore, the apostle must "lose" his life in order to recover it in the Holy Spirit. For the life that we manage to find on our own is one circumscribed and constricted by sin and selfishness. To attempt to find life apart from the assistance of the Holy Spirit remains a vain and venal pursuit limited to our unenlightened presumptions about the meaning of life and constrained by deficient notions of happiness and greatness.

However, to eschew self-centeredness in the holy hope of finding fulfillment in life beyond sense gratification is to claim life in the Spirit. The Blessed Virgin Mary, St. Joseph, St. John the Baptist, and Jesus himself are the exemplars of this Spirit-living in the Gospel of Matthew (Mt 1:18, 20; 3:11, 16; 4:1; 10:20; 12:18, 28, 31-32). And because the apostles are so intimately configured to the divine Trinity, they can with authority fulfill the command of the risen Christ to baptize the nations in the name of the Father, and of the Son, and of the Holy Spirit (Mt 28:19).

Conversely, if apostles faithfully embody the "prophetic" character of the Father who speaks the Word, the righteousness of Jesus Christ, and the littleness of the self-effacing Holy Spirit, then others will readily welcome the apostolic Church. In turn, they will receive the invaluable reward that accrues to those whose love, faith, and hope remain fixed wholly and completely on the Holy Trinity.

Fourteenth Sunday in Ordinary Time

The Revelation of the Father in Us
Matthew 11:25-30

Just as all Judea, Jerusalem, and the region around the Jordan confessed their sins to God before John the Baptist (Mt 3:6), so today Jesus confesses his praise of the Father in the presence of his disciples. Jesus rejoices because the Father reveals to little ones (Mt 21:16) knowledge of himself and of Christ as Son. This fact is confirmed later in the Gospel. After Peter declares Jesus to be the Messiah, the Son of the living God, the Lord replies by saying, "Flesh and blood has not revealed this to you, but my heavenly Father" (Mt 16:17). The Son wishes to reveal the Father, and, in Peter, the Father complies.

Thus, Jesus rejoices in the triumph of Gospel knowledge and understanding. Divine revelation breaks through the darkness of ignorance and transcends the limits of human rationality and the impairment of presumptions and of mistaken preconceptions. The dynamic of "hiddenness" is a key one in the spiritual life. Like the treasure buried in a field (Mt 13:44), the truth of the Father is hidden to the wise and the learned. The humility, docility, and obedience that distinguish the man who finds the treasure are the virtues that distinguish the "little ones" privileged to partake of the Father's revelation. These virtues protect the devoted disciple of Jesus from intimidation, so that what is concealed may be revealed, and the hidden known (Mt 10:26). And just as Jesus opens his mouth to announce what has lain hidden (Mt 13:35), so too does he expect us, not to hide the light of divine enlightenment, but rather to share it with the world (Mt 5:14). For the servant who hides what has been handed over to him by the Father will suffer the worst punishment (Mt 25:18, 30).

Unfortunately, many listen yet fail to understand (Mt 13:13-15, 19, 23). Just as the hardhearted did not recognize Elijah in the form of John the Baptist (Mt 17:12), so too are we at risk of not knowing the Son, and the Father whom he reveals, unless we remain his little ones. To do so, Jesus commands us to come to him. This call to "come" echoes Christ's call to his first disciples (Mt 4:18-22). It resounds the invitation to the wedding feast of the Kingdom (Mt 22:4). It grounds the foundation of faith in the Resurrection: "Come and see the place where he lay" (Mt 28:6). And it anticipates the call to inherit the Father's kingdom issued by Christ at the Second Coming (Mt 25:34). In short, in calling us to come to him, Jesus beckons us to take up our Christian vocation by making love of the Father's kingdom, faith in the Resurrection, and hope for ultimate communion in heaven the chief labor of our life and the source of our rest.

Moreover, to counteract life's struggles, we are to take up Christ's yoke, finding consolation in Christ's meekness. In this way, we identify with the lowly who are blessed (Mt 5:5), including Jesus himself (Mt 21:5). By preferring the humility of Jesus, we make ourselves lowly like the little children who rank with the greatest importance in the heavenly reign (Mt 18:4). Only the humility of Jesus that we freely take on predisposes us to grace-filled exaltation (Mt 23:12) precisely by freeing us from the harrowing burden of hypocrisy (Mt 23:4). If we insist on some self-serving excuse for not taking Christ's yoke upon us and learning from it, then what we have been given will be taken away (Mt 25:28).

For Jesus hands over to us what has been "handed over" to him by his Father: namely, his very self in death (Mt 17:22; 20:18-19; 26:2, 15, 16, 21, 23-25, 45, 46, 48; 27:2-4, 18, 26). When we embrace the goodness of the Father's "gracious will" hidden in the cross of Jesus Christ, we too give the Father praise worthy of the Son of God.

Fifteenth Sunday in Ordinary Time

The Seed of Faith, Hope, and Love
Matthew 13:1-23

What Jesus, in the midst of his temptations, first declared to the devil he drives home today by way of parable: "One does not live by bread alone, / but by every word that comes forth / from the mouth of God" (Mt 4:4). However, the reception of the Word resembles the beginning of bread: it begins as a seed. Careful diligence is needed to cultivate seed into wheat so that it may eventuate as bread. God's Word demands similar diligence.

Unfortunately, as the parable makes clear, people can be quite resistant to Christ's Word, for we prefer to live by our own word. Our "word" is basically the way we see the world, what we think is true. Our word concerns what we consider important, how we determine right from wrong, what we value, how we make assessments, decisions, choices, and so on. And our word frequently is at war with the Word of God. The Gospel warns us of three formidable threats to the seed of the Word of God taking root in our soul.

The first danger is that posed by the Evil One himself to those whose frantic lives remain so fixed on the "path" — the fast lane — that they fail to develop an abiding understanding or assimilation of the Word. Superficiality, activism, or any other disordered priority can keep us from taking the Word of God seriously. When we neglect to live by faith, the Evil One steals away God's Word, like ravenous birds eating up wayward seed. We need only listen to the Word of God to realize how much we should be wary of the Evil One (Mt 5:37; 6:13; 13:38). By listening attentively to the Word of God and living configured to it, we move off our own private paths and onto the Way who is Jesus.

Second, the Word withers in those who capitulate to the tribulation and persecution caused by the Word (like the third servant of the parable, Mt 25:18, 24-30). From the first moment of his preaching, the Word of God has predicted this persecution (Mt 5:10-11; 10:23). Jesus could not be clearer about the kind of tribulation the disciple should expect (Mt 24:9, 21, 29).

Falling away occurs when we give power to persecution, caving in to the intimidation of tribulation. However, the presence in our life of persecution, stemming from our obedience to God's Word, is in fact a confirmatory sign of blessedness. The Word of God itself safeguards us from falling away when confronted by conflict. "Blessed is the one who takes no offense at me" (Mt 11:6) — or in the suffering of the cross that necessarily attends our union with Christ. Even when nations hate us on account of Jesus Christ, we will not falter (Mt 24:10) because the Word of God fortifies our hope: "The one who perseveres to the end will be saved" (Mt 24:13). We see it first in our Gospel fruitfulness.

Finally, the third danger concerns misplaced love. The thorns represent worldly anxiety, such as Christ has already denounced (Mt 6:25-34), and the lure of riches. Such desires cannot coexist with the Word of God (Mt 6:24). Notice that the devil need not intervene himself in such cases, for those caught up in greed damn themselves (Mt 19:23-24). There is something suicidal about obsessing over anxiety and riches, for these vices themselves choke the Word of God. No wonder, then, that in sending out his Twelve Apostles to preach the Gospel, Jesus instructs them not to take along any gold, silver, or copper (Mt 10:9). For the witness of how confidently they love God's Word converts people, turning them away from lives of selfishness. When we are imbued with such single-hearted love for Jesus, the Word becomes the wheat that becomes the bread that becomes the Body of Christ.

SIXTEENTH SUNDAY IN ORDINARY TIME

WEEDS, MUSTARD SEED, AND LEAVEN
Matthew 13:24-43

If our primary priority vis-à-vis the Gospel is to seek first the Father's kingship over us and his way of holiness (Mt 6:33), then this becomes the pressing question: What will that search be like? What can we expect?

The Lord purifies our expectations today by making reference to weeds, mustard seed, and leaven.

The image of the mustard seed impresses upon us the instrumentality of hope in the process of justification. Being "the smallest of all the seeds," the mustard seed can readily be overlooked and disregarded. When discouraged by our own insignificance, inadequacy, and mediocrity, it is easy for us to misjudge our fittingness for the kingdom of heaven. Those opposed to the Gospel treacherously seize upon this insecurity. The ruthless world imposes its self-important standards upon all who will listen. The world aims to brainwash us into believing that we, with our many defects, limitations, and sins, are worthless in God's sight. It savagely angles to convince us that we cannot make any difference, thereby inculcating in us deadly self-doubt and despair. It connives to make us mistake our nothingness for nullification. Corrupted by such sordid criteria, we tragically misconstrue the preferences of Providence and underrate our progress in our relationship with God. For to seek the Father's kingship means believing in the potential he has planted within us that takes root through hope. When it comes to the Gospel, less is more. Littleness produces greatness.

Likewise, the leaven provides an invaluable lesson about love. Transformation happens when the yeast gets mixed with the three measures of wheat. In the same way, the situations of life become transformed by the quality of Gospel love that we invest in them. If the woman wants leavened bread, and not merely matzo, then she must make the deliberate, well-timed decision to add leaven to the mixture. In the same way, every circumstance of life presents us with an opportunity for making a con-

97

scious decision to choose charity instead of some lesser motive in all our thoughts, words, and dealings.

However, the one parable that the disciples fail to understand is that of the weeds and the wheat. We can sympathize because often we, too, fail to see the propitious role of evil in the process of our sanctification. Yet, our struggle with sin providentially effects in us authentic Gospel faith, for we can withstand the perilous battle between virtue and vice waged in our soul precisely by embracing the truth that God is in charge. God is the One who sustains us from moment to moment, loving us just the way we are right now. Thus, if the Lord permits some influence of the Evil One in our life, he does so because he knows it will intensify the personal adherence of our whole self to God.

Indeed, grace-guided interaction with iniquity perfects our holiness. It saves us from self-delusion as our confidence and trust in God grow in direct proportion to our knowledge of our misery without him. The presence of the weeds deepens our dependence on the mercy of God and liberates us from self-destructive self-reliance. Faith demands that sanctity heed God's method and schedule, not our own.

The punishment meted out to those who "cause others to sin and all evildoers" is categorically the worst – and often repeated! – in the Gospel of Matthew (Mt 8:12; 13:42, 50; 22:13; 24:51; 25:30). However, those who attain righteousness via the faith that recognizes the providential role of evil, the hope that remains focused on God's greatness and not human puniness, and the love that leavens every situation will "shine like the sun" with the same splendor of holiness as the transfigured Christ (Mt 17:2).

SEVENTEENTH SUNDAY IN ORDINARY TIME

INSTRUCTED IN THE KINGDOM
Matthew 13:44-52

The kingdom of heaven is the gathering around the Father of all those who belong to Jesus Christ and who live only for him. Today's Gospel addresses how to attain that kingdom. The three means revealed by Jesus may contradict our expectations. Accordingly, the Lord's purpose is to instruct us in the kingdom of heaven so that, like the resourceful scribe, we can bring from the storeroom of the Gospel both the new and the old in order to sustain and perfect our life of faith.

We need to read between Christ's lines in order to unlock the radical imperatives implied by these mini-parables. For example, a person of lesser character might simply steal the buried treasure he happens upon. However, the person in the parable, "out of joy," liquidates his assets in order to buy the field. His joy is not self-serving euphoria. Rather, it resembles the joy of the Magi (Mt 2:10), of those persecuted for Christ (Mt 5:12), of the one who hears God's Word (Mt 13:20), of the shepherd who finds his lost sheep (Mt 18:13), of the faithful servants (Mt 25:21, 23), and of the women at the Resurrection (Mt 28:8).

In other words, he possesses the joy of those who find Jesus and who live fully for him. The finder rejoices over the divine favor accorded him. He fittingly manifests his joy in a supreme act of self-sacrifice — his creative response to God's offer of mercy. In the gift of self that the man makes by selling all he has, he attains for himself what the rich man forfeits due to his egoistic refusal of the command of Christ (Mt 19:21-22). Desire for the Kingdom informs his moral actions. The unearthing of the Kingdom galvanizes in him the life of divine love.

Similarly, the merchant searching for fine pearls presumably knows what he is looking for. He has a standard of excellence in mind that nothing will make him compromise. Accordingly, when his quest leads him to discover "a pearl of great price," he, like the first man, "goes and sells all that he has" and buys it. Keep in mind that this venture entails an incalculable gamble. His assessment of the pearl's worth must be absolutely accurate because he cannot engage in such a transaction ever again. Once the merchant sells all he has, he loses all his fiscal leverage and collateral. To mistake what is truly valuable could cost the merchant his livelihood and even his life. This dynamic underscores how one arrives at the kingdom of heaven via a deliberate, self-committed search that entails taking great risks, but that resolves in the confidence of well-invested faith.

Finally, entrance into the kingdom of heaven belongs to the "righteous" like St. Joseph (Mt 1:19), the saints who endured the interaction of the Evil One (Mt 13:43), and the sheep who tend selflessly to the needy (Mt 25:37). In other words, the righteous are those who live by hope, taking great risks and making substantial sacrifices to put Jesus Christ first and to live only for him. The "wicked," on the other hand, bring their badness upon themselves by cultivating base habits and lifestyles that produce only rotten fruit (Mt 7:17-18; 12:33). We are thrown together in the net of the kingdom of heaven, but it is up to us how to respond to the offer of grace. In our accountability before God, recollection refines our freedom.

What if the buried treasure found by the man were the very one buried by the wicked third servant of the parable (Mt 25:18)? The servant would learn the hard way how imprudent his action was. By throwing away his chance to live for God's kingdom, he himself gets thrown away along with the wicked who wail and grind their teeth (Mt 25:30).

Eighteenth Sunday in Ordinary Time

Withdrawal and Satisfaction
Matthew 14:13-21

Jesus seeks the solace of solitude to assist him in his mourning over the death of John the Baptist, and so he withdraws to a deserted place. There is a pattern of "withdrawing" throughout Christ's life. Under the protection of Joseph, Jesus first withdraws to Egypt when threatened by the murderous Herod (Mt 2:14) and then to Nazareth (Mt 2:22). Jesus withdraws when he learns of the arrest of John the Baptist (Mt 4:12). He withdraws from the Pharisees when they plot to destroy him (Mt 12:15) and after debating with the Pharisees (Mt 15:21). In short, Jesus withdraws whenever evil imperils his fulfilling his Father's plan. Jesus' retreat intensifies his filial obedience and offers him new opportunities to manifest the Father's love.

Quite likely, Jesus desires some seclusion in a "deserted place" as he reflects on John the Baptist because the desert is where John began his ministry (Mt 3:1, 3; 11:7). There he can best recall the greatness of John. The desert is also where Christ underwent his temptations (Mt 4:1). Thus, the desert reminds Jesus of the self-donation of John the Baptist and his own total gift of self to the Father's will.

When Jesus Christ is present in the desert, a place of vast barrenness turns into a lavish banquet. Jesus' tender heart, all the more sensitized as a result of his grief over the loss of his friend and cousin John, is "moved with pity" (Mt 9:36; 15:32; 18:27; 20:34) when he sees the huge crowds. For they are true disciples, "following" Christ in faith wherever he ministers (Mt 4:25; 8:1; 12:15; 19:2; 20:29; 21:9), despite hardship, personal risk, and the possibility of never meeting Jesus.

However, the desert intimidates his closest disciples. They want Jesus to "dismiss" the crowds — a request they will repeat regarding others (Mt 15:23, 32). Nonetheless, Jesus takes advantage of this occasion of heartfelt loss and extreme need to reveal a key Gospel truth: "Give them some food yourselves." Christ's instruction foreshadows the command he will give to the grieving Peter after the Resurrection: "Feed my sheep" (Jn

21:17). Sometimes it takes the experience of being utterly bereft before we can realize the rich resources perpetually available to us through the presence of Jesus Christ. Dismissal is not the answer — deeper union with Jesus is. Thanks to the Incarnation, there is nowhere else to withdraw to.

For this reason, the Lord dismisses instead their suggestion that the crowds go to the villages to buy food for themselves. Christ's followers are to use their money to buy, not bread, but buried treasure (Mt 13:44), the truly valuable pearl (Mt 13:46), and oil for empty lamps (Mt 25:9, 10). In other words, Jesus endorses the expenditure of personal assets that enables one to seek first the kingdom of God and the Father's way of holiness. Then all other necessary things will be given to those who believe (Mt 6:33).

As for food, Jesus himself provides the miraculous meal that alone "satisfies." In the desolateness of this place, with nothing to look forward to but the power of Jesus, Christ's disciples are afforded a prime opportunity to hunger and thirst for holiness (Mt 5:6). Detached from lesser desires, they can — perhaps for the first time — savor the taste of true satisfaction. Christians are called to seek out others secluded in spiritual deserts and share the fragments of that satisfaction with the mourning and the hungry.

NINETEENTH SUNDAY IN ORDINARY TIME

THE ARK OF THE CHURCH
Matthew 14:22-33

Jesus makes his disciples get into the boat today in order to make them understand the importance of living by ecclesial faith. For the boat is a symbol of the Church. Jesus instructs his disciples to precede him in the boat in order to emphasize the extent to which faith must take precedence in the journey of life.

The act of "preceding" is a profoundly honorable one in the Gospel of Matthew. The star precedes the Magi, leading them to Jesus (Mt 2:9). The crowds precede Jesus in order to hail him during his triumphal entry into Jerusalem (Mt 21:9). The tax collectors and prostitutes precede the chief priests and elders into heaven (Mt 21:31). And Jesus himself precedes his apostles to Galilee after his Resurrection (Mt 26:32; 28:7). Preceding leads to glory.

Similarly, the multiplication of the loaves with which Jesus has just fed the people is a symbol of the Eucharist. The disciples in the boat must learn that, although Christ appears to be physically absent from them, through the effects of the Eucharist the Lord is always really present and active in their souls. Christians fed by the Church must live in confidence, relying on the Eucharist to sustain them.

Christ is not idle while he is away from his disciples. Rather, he goes up the mountain (or mount) to pray (Mt 14:23; 26:36-44). We witness Jesus going up out of the water after his baptism (Mt 3:16), going up the mountain to preach the Beatitudes (Mt 5:1), to heal the sick (Mt 15:29), and to be transfigured (Mt 17:1). Jesus goes up to Jerusalem to die (Mt 20:17-18). Thus, "going up" is a key action in Christ's fulfillment of his Father's will. After the terrifying episode on the waves today, Peter goes up into the boat — a sign that he is more fully disposed to carrying out the will of the Father united with Christ. Moreover, the Greek verb meaning "to go up" is redolent of the Ascension. These moments of separation when Jesus is on the mountain — these episodes of "going up" — prepare the disciples for that time in the near future when they will have to live their faith with steadfastness once Jesus has ascended into heaven.

The mountain is the preeminent place of temptation (Mt 4:8), divine revelation (Mt 5:1), Gospel witness (Mt 5:14), healing (Mt 8:1; 15:29), transfiguration (Mt 17:1), reconciliation (Mt 18:12), refuge (Mt 24:16), Resurrection (Mt 28:16), and of proving the power of faith (Mt 17:20; 21:21). Thus, Christ's presence in prayer on the mountain is as dynamic and effective for the disciples in the boat as Christ's Real Presence in the tabernacle.

Just as God tried the Israelites in the desert, so the Lord tests his disciples on the sea. A clue to this is indicated where the Gospel says that the waves tossed them about – a Greek verb that literally means "to suffer" (see its use in Mt 4:24; 8:6; 18:34). Yet, the disciples have already seen Jesus calm a storm at sea (Mt 8:23-27). Nonetheless, they remain of "little faith" (Mt 6:30; 8:26; 13:58; 16:8; 17:17, 20; 21:25, 32). In their state of being "terrified," they resemble King Herod (Mt 2:3). Christ has already proclaimed how deleterious and even reprehensible such fear is (Mt 10:26-31).

Peter asks for a command from Jesus that attests to Christ's identity. And well he should, for one word reveals Jesus as Savior (Mt 8:8; 15:28). When Peter persists in his doubt (Mt 28:17), Jesus stretches out his hand – a gesture of restoration (Mt 8:3; 12:13), of initiation (Mt 12:49), and ultimately of ordination. The preceding time Jesus walked along the Sea of Galilee it was to call his first disciples (Mt 4:18). Now as Jesus walks on the sea, he quickens and advances Peter's divine vocation. The first duty of those in the boat remains our own: to worship (Mt 2:2, 11; 8:2; 28:9, 17) the Son of God (Mt 27:43, 54).

TWENTIETH SUNDAY IN ORDINARY TIME

WHAT MAKES FAITH GREAT
Matthew 15:21-28

If the little girl in today's Gospel is so desperately sick, then why isn't her mother home by her side? Jesus himself declares that if anyone wishes to come after him, he must deny his very self, take up his cross, and begin to follow in his footsteps (Mt 16:24). According to Mark's recounting, this event happens inside a house (Mk 7:24-30). However, in Matthew's version, it takes place outside on the road. The Canaanite woman literally follows in Jesus' footsteps, selflessly taking up the cross of her anguish. Jesus insists, "Whoever loves . . . son or daughter more than me is not worthy of me" (Mt 10:37). The mother proves by her discipleship how much her love for Jesus is the first priority in her life. It is that unmitigated love for Christ that will make her worthy of the healing she requests for her daughter.

Christ has already shown the pity for which the woman pleads, in his healing of the two blind men (Mt 9:27-29), and he will soon show it to the father of the possessed boy (Mt 17:15, 18) as well as to the blind men of Jericho (Mt 20:30-31). In other words, Christ offers his pity to those without vision and to those in the grip of the Enemy. The plea for Christ's pity is an act of faith that confesses his divinity. The reception of Christ's pity effects Gospel piety.

Yet, Jesus says not a word in response to the woman's request. Jesus will also remain silent before the high priest (Mt 26:62-63) and before Pilate (Mt 27:12, 14). Jesus' antagonists ask questions in an attempt to defy and denounce Christ's authority. But the woman "keeps calling out"; her pious persistence salutes the Lord's supremacy.

Nevertheless, by what right do we dare approach the Lord of the universe to beseech his aid? Jesus claims that he has been sent to the lost sheep of the house of Israel. Yet today he is far away from Jerusalem in Tyre and Sidon, practically in pagan territory (Mt 10:5-6). And is not this woman, as she follows in Christ's footsteps, like the one who loses his life in order to gain it (Mt 10:39; 16:25)? In many ways, she is the very model of the lost sheep whom Jesus the Good Shepherd pities and seeks out (Mt 9:36; 18:10-14). Her posture of supplication and homage (Mt 2:2, 8, 11; 8:2; 9:18; 14:33; 20:20; 28:9, 17) bespeaks her holy predisposition.

When the Lord rejoins with yet another seeming objection, the undaunted woman responds with pure deference, reverence, and finesse. It is right for her to be there, like the apostles at the Transfiguration (Mt 17:4), and to receive the scraps from the table because she truly hungers and thirsts for holiness (Mt 5:6). The food that she solicits is not bread alone (Mt 4:4) but rather the daily bread (Mt 6:11) that is an extension of divine revelation — the utterance that comes from the mouth of God. The fact that she calls Jesus "Son of David" (Mt 1:1; 9:27; 12:23; 20:30-31; 21:9, 15; 22:42-43) testifies to her great confidence in God's fidelity to the promises he made to King David (even though she herself is not Jewish) — a fidelity now incarnate in Jesus Christ.

Unlike many others, this woman has looked at Jesus and seen, has heard and understood (Mt 13:13-15). Therefore, Jesus extols the woman's "great faith" (Mt 8:10-13; 9:2; 9:28-29; 18:6; 21:21-22). Christ heals the woman's daughter in an act of re-creation with the words "let it be done" — the root of "genesis" (see also Mt 8:13; 9:29; 18:19; 21:21; 26:42). In calling the mother "woman," Jesus identifies her both with the first woman, Eve, and with the New Eve, Mary, whom Jesus addresses as "woman" from the cross (Jn 19:26).

Twenty-First Sunday in Ordinary Time

Saying Who Jesus Is
Matthew 16:13-20

Christ asks the critical question: "Who do you say that I am?" The question is more formidable than it may seem. Pope John Paul II wrote that "we need now more than ever to have the courage to look the truth in the eye and to call things by their proper name, without yielding to convenient compromises or to the temptation of self-deception." The disciples in reply come up with many seemingly apt appellations: John the Baptist, Elijah, Jeremiah, a prophet. But all of these names fall short of the true identity of Jesus Christ. In settling for these descriptions, one tempts self-deception by overlooking the salvific objective of the Incarnation. For to say who Jesus is requires that we confess who we are: helpless sinners in need of redemption. To call Jesus "the Christ" means that we must become Christians.

Thus, the Truth looks Peter in the eye and restates his question. Through the posing of his question, Jesus invites us to perfection. Human beings become complete when they reach out infinitely beyond themselves and unite themselves to Jesus Christ. We become more fully human the less we are obsessed with self and enclosed in ego. The Father himself reveals to Peter the relationship that defines Jesus: he is the Son of God. His anointing as "Christ" flows from that union of Father and Son. Thus, Christ is not merely a political messiah, but the one true Messiah whose anointing can enable us to reach beyond ourselves to the infinite. In Jesus Christ, we can seek first the kingship and holiness of the Father. At the Transfiguration (Mt 17:5), the Father will confirm the revelation that he has made to Peter.

Moreover, when we redirect the energy that we formerly spent on egoism to the Savior, conforming ourselves radically to Jesus Christ, our life changes profoundly. When we embrace the grace of self-forgetfulness and stop thinking about self, then we for the first time realize how much God thinks of us, and how that merciful mindfulness transforms us. Cardinal Joseph Ratzinger quotes an author who rightly revises the Cartesian formula "I think, therefore I am" to "I am thought, therefore I am." By courageously confessing the Messiahship and Sonship of Jesus Christ, our very being changes.

We witness this Gospel transformation in "Simon" today. Once Simon makes his confession — "You are the Christ, the Son of the living God" — Jesus gives him a new name: "Peter." Peter's new name signifies that he is no longer the sum total of his failures, sorrows, sins, missed chances, heartbreaks, anger, bad moods, hopelessness, and any other inadequacy that plagues people outside of Christ. When we confess the identity of Jesus, we in turn are blessed with a new identity. We escape the stranglehold of egoism and individualism. Configured to Jesus Christ, we can never again say "I am" apart from him.

But where today do we find the wherewithal to look truth in the eye and to call things by their proper names? Jesus knows all too well the weak human inclination to remake the Messiah according to a worldly image. He knows how readily compromised and self-deceived hearts would reduce the Son of God to nothing more than a wise man or wonderworker. And so he builds his Church upon the Rock of Peter. Through the Magisterium of Peter, we can confidently look Truth in the eye. Through the consolation of the Keys — the Sacrament of Penance — we resist the presumption whereby we would yield to convenient compromises. Enclosed not in our own egos but in the embrace of the Church, we have not only the courage to withstand even the assault of the netherworld but also the wisdom to call things by their proper names. We see the presence and primacy of Jesus Christ in everything.

TWENTY-SECOND SUNDAY IN ORDINARY TIME

THINKING AS GOD DOES
Matthew 16:21-27

Today Jesus begins to "show" his disciples that he must suffer greatly. Peter interprets this "showing" in much the same way that Jesus understands the showing he experienced from a high mountain in the desert of all the world's magnificent kingdoms: as a temptation of the devil (Mt 4:8). However, it is Peter himself who voices the sentiments of the tempter in the form of a "rebuke." On other occasions, the disciples rebuke children to keep them from approaching Jesus (Mt 19:13), and the crowds rebuke the two shouting blind men of Jericho in order to silence them (Mt 20:31). Their rebuking would prohibit Jesus from bestowing his mercy. Ironically, Peter's rebuke, "God forbid!" literally means "God be merciful." Yet, that mercy is precisely what his misguided rebuke impedes.

Elsewhere in the Gospel of Matthew, Jesus himself rebukes the winds and the sea (Mt 8:26), the crowds who want to make public his healings (Mt 12:16), his disciples to keep them from revealing that he was the Messiah (Mt 16:20), and the demon in the possessed boy (Mt 17:18). In other words, Christ's rebukes are ordered to perfecting faith.

Thus, we can appreciate the severity of Christ's "turning" (cf. Mt 9:22) to Peter. Jesus reprimands Peter in the same way that he reprimanded Satan himself in the temptation (Mt 4:10) and in the demons of Gadara (Mt 8:32). The obstacle posed by Peter rivals the enormity caused by scandal (Mt 18:6-9). To "forbid" the Passion is to deny mercy at its very source. There is nothing more satanic in the world.

Thus, the lesson that Jesus has already taught his disciples about losing one's life in order to discover it (Mt 5:29-30; 10:39) can at last be fully understood. For it is impossible to comprehend the Gospel doctrine of self-abnegation without the light of the cross. Thanks to today's first Passion prediction, the wisdom and goodness of self-renunciation can be grasped with genuine fervor and confidence. Just as the healed leper must show himself to the priest in order to prove the divine source of his cure (Mt 8:4), so Jesus shows us in advance the horrors of his own wounds on Calvary in order to convince us of the reality of redemption. Failure to embrace active denial of self festers into the blasphemous and death-dealing denial of Jesus Christ (Mt 10:33; 26:34, 35, 70, 72, 74).

Accordingly, we must "take up" (Mt 9:6; 11:29; 14:20 15:37; 27:32) our cross or else risk having the gift of divine life taken away from us (Mt 25:28-29). There is no profit in attempting to gain anything apart from the providence of the Father, as the parable of the talents illustrates so poignantly (Mt 25:16-22). However, if we follow Jesus, especially through our obedience to what he reveals, then we will "find" rest (Mt 11:29), treasure (Mt 13:44), happiness (Mt 18:13), companionship (Mt 27:32), and what we seek (Mt 7:7-8) — in short, the fullness of life. The Father will repay (Mt 6:4, 6, 18) conduct ("praxis") that conforms us to the cross of his Son.

When the Son of Man returns with his angels in his Father's glory, he will be looking for disciples who think, not like worldly human beings, but as God himself (Mt 25:31-40). With that Gospel frame of mind, the reasonableness and the beauty of the Passion make complete sense.

Twenty-Third Sunday in Ordinary Time

The Power of Two or Three
Matthew 18:15-20

The penetrating directives that Jesus gives today regarding sinners indicate how fully apprised he is of the imbroglio of sin. The Lord addresses three stages of sin. The first is the imprudent commission of an actual offense against another. Next, the sin becomes convoluted when the sinner, unmoved by the correction offered by the offended one, rejects any culpability for his sin. The sin then gets further attenuated and aggravated when the sinner rejects the testimony of two or three witnesses. Finally, isolated sin blossoms into full-blown, blasphemous self-righteousness when the sinner refuses to listen even to the Church.

This pernicious pattern of sin is all too familiar to us. Very often, it is not a particular sin itself but rather the lies that we concoct around our sin that escalate its gravity, thereby undermining our moral rectitude. The devil exploits our egoistic vanity in order to wreak this spiritual sabotage in our would-be innocent, actually insolent soul.

The heavenly power that Christ bestows upon his Church to bind and loose sin provides the only sanctified dynamic for escaping the diabolical predicament of sin. Christ makes the method for quelling the quandary of sin concrete in the Sacrament of Penance because he knows how much we rely on the graced counsel of another to preserve the communion of faith. Pope John Paul II confirmed this when he wrote that "the confession of sins corresponds to that legitimate and natural need, inherent in the human heart, to open oneself to another." In short, Jesus Christ does not resort to miracles or other spectacular means to reconcile sinners. Rather, he relies on the reasonableness of Gospel faith to counter the dilemma of sin. In the charitable encounter with another, we hear Truth speaking.

The key to the reception of Gospel mercy is the willingness to listen to the truth. For if we are not listening to the truth, we are invariably listening to our own ideas and understanding, our own conception of right and wrong, our own revision of reality. As today's Gospel paradigm points out, such delusional deception expects everyone else — including the Church — actually to condone and sanction the sinner's sin. Yet, Jesus makes perfectly clear that we are never to be complicit in the iniquity of others. Christ has already specified the severe way that the Twelve are to deal with those who refuse to listen to the Gospel (Mt 10:14). God will not coerce the freedom of hearers. Those who refuse the mercy meted out by the Sacred Penitentiary of the Church due to their own obstinacy, intractability, or dissent remain responsible for the disastrous consequences of their disobedience.

The Church teaches that the presence of five conditions determines when a Christian has the obligation to extend fraternal correction to an erring neighbor. First, the transgression must involve serious matter. Second, there must be a real necessity for fraternal correction, such as when the offender is unwilling to correct himself. Third, the correction must do no harm while at the same time maintaining reasonable hope that the offender will realize the usefulness of the correction and heed it. Fourth, any risks assumed in correction must be proportioned to the neighbor's need, keeping in mind that fear of offense or anger is not a legitimate excuse for refusing to correct another. And finally, the correction must be done in charity at a suitable opportunity, avoiding unwarranted embarrassment and publicity. St. Augustine observes that the sorrow prompted by fraternal correction can serve as the very catalyst needed to spawn the desire for repentance and reform in the offender.

This communal power extends to prayer as well (Mt 9:27-29; 17:1; 20:29-34; 26:37), saving us from self-deceiving individualism, manipulation, and "privatized" faith.

TWENTY-FOURTH SUNDAY IN ORDINARY TIME

FORGIVENESS FROM THE HEART
Matthew 18:21-35

"Enough is enough" is not a sentiment shared by Jesus Christ, especially when it comes to forgiveness. Peter suggests imposing a seven-time stipulation on the offer of forgiveness. Yet, Jesus insists on unrestricted liberality regarding forgiveness. Christ makes clear that forgiveness cannot be occasional but must remain constant. For the instant that we withhold forgiveness is the moment we forget that we have been forgiven. Forgiveness is absolutely indispensable to Gospel living. Forgiveness keeps us focused on divine mercy. In short, forgiveness is the concrete way we seek first the Father's kingship and his way of holiness.

Thus, the Lord's parable today reveals the kind of heart we must possess in order to fulfill the command to forgive. Christ warns sternly against those who harbor evil in their hearts (Mt 9:4), those whose hearts are sluggish (Mt 13:15), those whose hearts are distant from God (Mt 15:8), those whose hearts are filled with evil designs (Mt 15:19), and those whose hearts are ruled by obstinacy (Mt 19:8). Forgiveness means nothing to those polluted by defective hearts. In rendering forgiveness null and void, they drain life of its vitality.

However, forgiveness comes easily to the single-hearted (Mt 5:8; 22:37), for the desire to forgive forms the prayer of the pure of heart (Mt 6:12). The logic of reciprocity in forgiveness assures them of the genuineness of reconciliation (Mt 6:14-15). Offering forgiveness to another is not about working up will power, but rather about extending the divine power of Jesus Christ to another by virtue of one's graced union with him (Mt 9:2, 5, 6). Participation in the Eucharist assures our ability to forgive others, especially when we feel as if it is the last thing we can do (Mt 26:28). It protects us from the seduction of presumption.

Conversely, the only sin that will not be forgiven is the sin against the Holy Spirit that posits the impotency of mercy and forgiveness (Mt 12:31-32). Those who espouse this blasphemy cannot be forgiven because they never ask for forgiveness. On the other hand, those who truly understand the abomination of evil, the utter helplessness of life without God, and the redemptive might of mercy remain ever eager to forgive.

In effect, the parable is the Lord's Prayer in action. Although the debtor (Mt 6:12) owes the king a vast fortune, the king is moved with compassion because the man demonstrates seemingly sincere reverence and piety. The compassion of the king resembles that of Christ toward the exhausted crowds (Mt 9:36; 14:14; 15:32) and toward the two blind men (Mt 20:34). Such obeisance means more to him than the immense debt that he forgives.

Yet, we immediately witness the servant's deceitfulness. Before the fellow servant who owes him a mere pittance can even say a word, the wicked one literally embodies the lure of money by choking him (cf. Mt 13:7, 22). Moreover, the abused servant begs with words that mimic those of the wicked servant himself. The Greek term for *beg* shares the same root with the word for *Paraclete*. Others petition Christ in this way — the centurion (Mt 8:5), the Gadarene demons (Mt 8:31), and the people seeking to touch his cloak (Mt 14:36) — and Jesus willingly accedes to each request. But the wicked servant refuses — an unwillingness that recalls the guests who refuse the king's invitation (Mt 22:3) and Jerusalem at the time of its visitation (Mt 23:37). In his hypocritical perversion, it is sacrifice he desires, not mercy (cf. Mt 9:13; 12:7). Even worse, the servant's ruthlessness "disturbs" the very peace of the community.

To live without pity (Mt 5:7) makes us pitiful. Christ will soon excoriate the scribes and Pharisees for neglecting mercy and good faith (Mt 23:23). Only our preeminent esteem of forgiveness saves us from the torture that heartlessness would visit upon us.

Twenty-Fifth Sunday in Ordinary Time

The Justice of Heaven
Matthew 20:1-16a

We cannot gain the kingdom of heaven if we do not empathize with the landowner of today's parable, who embodies the Kingdom. He models the mercy of the Kingdom in the persistence with which he personally goes out into the marketplace to hire laborers for his vineyard. The landowner's unfailing initiative exemplifies the solicitude of the Father, who never ceases to draw us to himself through his Son. The hours of his search match the hours of prayer. Moreover, dawn is the time when the chief priests meet in council about Jesus (Mt 27:1). Noon is when the darkness of Good Friday begins (Mt 27:45). And three o'clock is when Jesus cries out from the cross (Mt 27:45-46). Thus, the salvific import of the landowner's ministrations appears in his timing; they coincide with key moments of the Passion.

The landowner's question to the laborers he meets late in the day is not an obvious one: "Why do you stand here idle all day?" For it gives the workers the opportunity to express their unfailing *desire to work*. At that late hour, lesser men would have given up any hope of being hired, either out of fatigue or out of despondency. But that desire, that obedient responsiveness to the commission of the Vine-grower, makes them worthy of heaven. For the true "work" of the Christian is obeying the will of the Father. The laborers appreciate the value of spending even just one hour at work in the vineyard, and they gratefully seize it.

Those who grumble against the landowner, however, miss the whole point. How they resemble the detestable ingrate who throttles a fellow servant and demands, "Pay back what you owe" (Mt 18:28). His refusal to abide by mercy lands him in prison. The grumblers complain that the landowner has made the workers hired late equal to them. But in reality, the landowner, through the offer of mercy, has made them equal *to himself!* The complainers have forgotten that, without the generosity of the landowner, they would all still be standing idle in the marketplace. Jesus warns that on Judgment Day people will be held accountable for every idle word they speak (Mt 12:36). These presumptuous words of the grumblers are what Jesus has in mind. That is the only "account" they should be concerned about.

In retort, the landowner addresses the spokesman as "friend": an ominous term in the Gospel of Matthew used only of the exploitative, expelled wedding guest (Mt 22:12) and Judas (Mt 26:50) — that is, those who repudiate and even betray the invitation of the kingdom of heaven. If the early workers were to accuse the landowner of cheating them, they would also have to accuse God of being a cheat for having the rain fall on the just and the unjust alike (Mt 5:45). The freedom of the kingdom of heaven cannot be assessed by unredeemed earthly justice. The landowner is as free to do what he likes with his money as Jesus is free to cure on the Sabbath (Mt 12:10). In choosing to give the last the same as the first, the landowner identifies with the virtuous choosing of St. Joseph (Mt 1:19). The inability of the grumblers to grasp this demonstrates how the one who chooses his life loses it (Mt 16:25).

Ineluctably, envy disqualifies presumptuous, self-righteous grumblers from the kingdom of heaven. For they fail to see how every one of us is a worker hired late. No one has a claim to the resources of the Father. Nobody can earn his way into heaven. And if God deems to be more generous with others than he is with us, it is simply because the others are more in need of his mercy. "Envy" is literally an "evil eye" that must be torn out (Mt 5:29; 18:9) because it blinds us to the generosity of God and keeps us from delighting in the mercy of the Kingdom. The Lord gives us a second chance to revise the way we think about late laborers (Mt 21:28-31) and vineyard workers in dealing with the gift of a son (Mt 21:37-39).

TWENTY-SIXTH SUNDAY IN ORDINARY TIME

CHANGING OUR MIND
Matthew 21:28-32

Perhaps the most important word in the whole Gospel passage to-day is one inconspicuous little adverb: "afterwards." The use of this Greek word to signify a change of mind occurs only one other time in the Gospel of Matthew: in the description of Judas' regret at betraying Jesus (Mt 27:3). Thus, the mind-set that Christ inquires about today is a critical one. Like the ill-prepared bridesmaids who return "afterwards" for the wedding banquet (Mt 25:11), we may find it is too late when we finally get around to changing our mind to God's way of thinking. An avoidable mistake in judgment can exclude us from the feast. As in the case of Judas, even well-intentioned remorse, if it is last-minute, may not be able to prevent our undoing. Clearly, the opinions we hold may be a matter of life or death — for ourselves and for others.

Several times in the Gospel, Jesus asks this question: "What is your opinion?" (Mt 17:25; 18:12; 22:42). In each instance, the question intends to clarify misconceptions about the identity of Jesus and to reinforce the reach of the Father's mercy. For our opinion determines to what degree we reverence the "Father's will." From the first moment of his teaching, Jesus accentuates the primacy of doing the Father's will (Mt 6:10). For fulfilling the Father's will is the prerequisite for entrance into heaven (Mt 7:21). Our devotion to the will of the Father makes us brothers and sisters of Jesus (Mt 12:50). The Father's will pervades every instant of life and is solicitous toward the littlest ones of the Kingdom (Mt 18:14). It carries us through the darkest, most unbearable moments — as it did for Jesus (Mt 26:42) — enabling us to accomplish the seemingly impossible. Thus, it is essential for Christians to maintain an unwavering zeal about the Father's will, which must remain in the forefront of our mind from moment to moment.

We do the Father's will by going out and working in the vineyard when asked. In the Gospel of Matthew, the vineyard is a place where what one would least expect happens. In the vineyard, laborers who work for only an hour get paid the same amount as those who put in a full day (Mt 20:1-16). The vineyard is also the locus of murderous treachery leveled against a son intent upon carrying out his father's will (Mt 21:37-39). And the vineyard provides the drink for the Son once he enters into his Father's reign (Mt 26:29). The vineyard challenges and even overturns our worldly notions of justice. The suffering of the vineyard is inescapable, and the satisfaction of its fruit is everlasting.

The Father commands us to "go out" to "work" (Mt 9:37; 10:10; 20:1, 2, 8) in the vineyard, but the Father goes out himself again and again in search of those willing to do his work (Mt 20:4, 7, 14). It is the mercy of that divine initiative that revolutionizes our understanding of justice and that endows us with the mind of God. The "way of righteousness" that clearly forms the conscience of the first son, who changes his mind in favor of his father's will, is evident all around us. We need simply be attentive to those who hunger and thirst for it (Mt 5:6), who are willing to be persecuted for its sake (Mt 5:10), who surpass the scribes and Pharisees in their authenticity of life (Mt 5:20), and who seek the Father's kingship before all else (Mt 6:33).

In short, there is ample witness to the way of righteousness in the world. Only self-willed obstinacy and obduracy keep us from believing. And the refusal to change our mind when grace is plain to see puts us at the end of the line when it comes to entering into the kingdom of God. If we manage to get in at all, it will only be afterwards.

Twenty-Seventh Sunday in Ordinary Time

Respect and Inheritance
Matthew 21:33-43

The father sends his son as an emissary to the depraved tenants of his vineyard on the supposition that they care about decency: "They will respect my son." For what on earth surpasses the sacred bond between father and son? What union is more deserving of reverence – a union that images that of the Blessed Trinity? The brutality of the parable is meant to incite outrage in us over the blasphemy we commit regularly due to our impiousness toward God the Father. Such impiety occurs more easily than we may think.

Indeed, the savage response of the tenants confirms a crucial insight of Pope John Paul II: "Original sin attempts to abolish fatherhood, destroying the rays that permeate the created world." The tenants think that if they can destroy the son, then they can also abolish the father's hold over his vineyard. They presume that their barbarity will completely devastate the father, paving the way for them to co-opt the son's inheritance. In this way, they represent those who seek the Father's kingdom while repudiating his kingship.

But Jesus is quite exacting about who will inherit the Kingdom. The Kingdom is promised to those who are meek and lowly (Mt 5:5; 18:1-4). Yet the wretched tenants are as haughty and contemptuous as they come. Moreover, a prerequisite for inheriting everlasting life is the willingness to give up home, family, and property for Jesus' sake (Mt 19:29). However, these dastardly tenants try to do just the opposite: ruthlessly to take away the home, family, and property of the landowner. In addition, only those who are compassionately solicitous toward the hungry and thirsty, the alienated, the naked, the ill, and the imprisoned will inherit the Kingdom (Mt 25:34). The tenants, on the other hand, deliberately inflict even worse afflictions on those they encounter.

But the father does not take this atrocity lying down. Like those who make little of the great benefits offered them (Mt 13:12; 25:29), the kingdom of God will be taken away from those who abuse the gift of the

Son of God. Throughout his ministry, Jesus preaches the imperative of personal fruitfulness (Mt 3:8, 10; 7:17, 19). Attempting to steal the produce of others is like trying to steal their virtues. Rather, the tenants' chance in the vineyard closely resembles the golden opportunity that the master affords to his servants when he hands over his talents to them. The fruitfulness expected of those who will be given the Kingdom resembles that of the first servant (Mt 25:16).

Keep in mind, the sending of the son to the vineyard is not simply an analogy for the Incarnation. Rather, it signifies every time and every way that the Father sends his Son into our life. Which means it signifies every moment of our life. Every occasion of our life is a prime opportunity to exercise our obedience, our worship, and our piety toward the Father. That is the source of our fruitfulness. We need to be sensitive to the divine presence of the Son — in the sacraments, in the Word of God, in the sacred assembly, in God's priests, in our neighbor, and so on — in order to avoid the daily, tyrannizing temptation to try to seize God's kingdom without God. When we refuse such hospitality toward the Son of God in our midst, sacrilege can arise subtly and inconspicuously, resulting in our own destruction.

In short, the key for avoiding the calamity of the vicious tenants is a truth that has already been revealed by Jesus: "Whoever receives one child such as this in my name receives me" (Mt 18:5). The moment a disrespectful spirit takes over our soul is the time to take refuge in the Cornerstone until insolence gives way to humility.

Twenty-Eighth Sunday in Ordinary Time

The Wedding Feast and the Worthy Guest
Matthew 22:1-14

Today's parable concerns a king who invites guests to a wedding feast for his son. The first mention of a king in the Gospel of Matthew refers to the infant Jesus (Mt 2:2). From the moment of his birth, he too is rejected, this time by another king, Herod. The other king featured in a parable demonstrates tremendous pity and forgiveness — a compassion that the receiver promptly exploits (Mt 18:27-35). At the Last Judgment, Jesus the King will come as a shepherd to welcome into heaven those devoted to caring for needy neighbors in their affliction (Mt 25:34, 40). In his arraignment before Pilate and in his crucifixion, it is the kingship of Christ that gets contested, mocked, and rejected (Mt 27:11, 29, 37, 42). Thus, to rebuff the invitation of the king signifies a deadly and death-dealing lack of compassion. It denotes a refusal to accept the grace that the wedding feast represents.

Notice that the king's only request is that his guests *be there* at the feast. Nonetheless, catering instead to self-serving motives, they all callously — even murderously — decline the king's gracious invitation. Their refusal is not simply disobedience of duty owed the king; it is a repulsion of love (symbolized by the wedding) in favor of self-glorifying rationalization. The divine King desires our presence at the feast, not for his sake, but for our own good! Yet, those who disdain the wedding feast do so because they prefer to remain caught up in their own self-love. Those who live preoccupied by the "me" mentality have no desire to enter into the love of others. Their flagrant self-absorption remains an affront that signals a categorical disregard for both the king's son and the covenant signified by the wedding.

Cardinal Christoph Schönborn has written that "the Church is identified with Christ her Bridegroom, who is himself the kingdom. . . . If one were to abandon it, countless abuses in thought and deed would be the result." But the unworthy wedding guests commit just such abandonment today. To be "worthy" means to live with self-abandoned reliance on the providence of God (Mt 10:9-10). It means loving Jesus Christ more than father, mother, son, or daughter (Mt 10:37). To be worthy, we must be willing to take up our cross and follow after Jesus (Mt 10:38). The wedding feast prefigures the Last Supper: Christ's unending invitation to unite our sacrifices to his Paschal sacrifice so that they might be transformed through the Redemption. To unite ourselves to Christ's sacrifice means making the sacrifice of self-renunciation.

The king expels the man not dressed in a wedding garment because of his willfulness. The wedding garment signifies baptism and the sacraments – i.e., the sacred way we unite ourselves to Christ's Paschal sacrifice. The Gospel leads us to assume that the host provides the wedding garment for the man, but that the man obstinately discards it. Such insubordination is tantamount to betrayal, which is why the king addresses the ingrate in the same way that Jesus addresses Judas: "Friend" (Mt 26:50). The absence of any good excuse on the man's part confirms his guilt. He is reduced to silence, like the Sadducees by Jesus (Mt 22:34). And like the wicked third servant (Mt 25:30) – another symbol of Judas – the king casts him into the darkness where there is grinding of teeth (the kind of place that appeals only to out-of-work dentists).

Everything about the feast is ready, therefore we too must be ready (Mt 3:3; 24:44; 25:10). Our glory consists in knowing that God has chosen us (Mt 24:31) and in responding to his invitation by our faithful Sunday participation in the wedding feast of the Mass.

Twenty-Ninth Sunday in Ordinary Time

What Belongs to God
Matthew 22:15-21

You do not have to be divine to see through flattery. Anyone empty of egoism can readily distinguish earnestness from adulation. Jesus easily pierces the subterfuge of the dissembling delegates of the Pharisees. In fact, their flattery is mortally sinful because it malevolently intends to deceive Jesus in order to injure him in soul and, ultimately, body. St. Thomas Aquinas identifies flattery as a chief enemy of friendship. And our friendship is "what belongs to God." These hypocrites contrive to discredit this Gospel truth.

Jesus had run into this kind of "malice" before. He reads the evil thoughts of the scribes in Capernaum (Mt 9:4). And he deplores the evil, unfaithful age because of its eagerness for a sign (Mt 12:39, 45; 16:4). Yet, these conspirators, through their machinations, are after just that: a self-indicting sign with which to accuse and condemn Jesus Christ.

More specifically, the spiteful impostors hope to incite some incriminating evidence by baiting Jesus with a debate about politics and religion. In civil and moral matters, the world out of hand dismisses Christians as being backward, naïve, inept, quaint, and clueless. But woe to the one who schemes to entrap in speech the eternal Word of God. In his masterful retort, Jesus reveals the wisdom with which he imbues the Church — one that trounces worldly thinking and stifles its conniving.

The Second Vatican Council well expresses the mind of Christ about repaying what is due to Caesar:

> It is a mistake to think that . . . we are entitled to shirk our
> earthly responsibilities. . . . But it is no less mistaken to
> think that we may immerse ourselves in earthly activities
> as if these latter were utterly foreign to religion. . . . One
> of the gravest errors of our time is the dichotomy between
> the faith which many profess and the practice of their daily
> lives. . . . The Christian who shirks his temporal duties

shirks his duties towards his neighbor, neglects God himself, and endangers his eternal salvation (*Gaudium et Spes*, 43).

St. John counsels that "if anyone comes to you and does not bring [the teaching of Christ], do not receive him into your house or even greet him" (2 Jn 10). But Jesus does receive these hypocrites – and us who at times are like them – so that the splendor of the truth will unseat the mendacity of their hearts. By exposing their contemptuous masquerade on their terms, Christ intends to engage their warped but working reason in order to shepherd them to faith. He gives them a chance to see for themselves just how absurd their conspiracy is.

As an essential part of our Gospel mission, Jesus blesses us with that same ability. Christ empowers his disciples to meet the smugness, skepticism, criticism, and duplicity of the world. But we can do so only if we fully belong to God as Christians. That belonging remains characterized by uncompromising honesty and truthfulness, humble self-forgetfulness, and a heartfelt commitment to love Jesus the Teacher and "the way of God" that he reveals. It means opting for integrity over intrigue, for confidence over chicanery.

Jesus Christ knows everything that one needs to know about the relations between church and state. But even more, he knows the deepest intentions and motives of our heart, no matter how much we may try to hide them, no matter how vindictive they may be. Christ's encounter with these frauds is the Lord's way of saying, "Dump the deceitfulness of the Pharisees and find yourselves new friends."

THIRTIETH SUNDAY IN ORDINARY TIME

HEART, SOUL, MIND
Matthew 22:34-40

This is the third time that the Pharisees attempt to test Jesus (cf. Mt 16:1; 19:3). Their duplicity takes the form of a seemingly harmless question: "Which commandment in the law is the greatest?" We answer this question in our own lives by the way that we live. If we find in our lives a preponderance of selfishness, anger, jealousy, resentment, vindictiveness, greed, impurity, pettiness, impatience, self-righteousness, fear, loneliness, despair, or the desire to "get even" with others, then that is the greatest commandment for us.

Yet, Jesus declares that the greatest commandment is loving God with all our heart, soul, and mind. In reality, it is impossible for us unaided to love God and others the way that they must be loved. We can only love them that way if we love them with the love of Jesus. And the only way that we can love them with the love of Jesus is if Jesus gives us his love with which to love others.

In short, we can only love God the way he demands when we believe that God loves us, and when we live out of that love. When we know that we are loved, then we know how to love, and then we become completely loving.

Jesus instructs us to love God with all our heart, soul, and mind because that is how he proves his love for us. To love others with all our heart (cf. Mt 5:8, 28; 6:21; 12:34; 13:19; 15:8, 18-19; 18:35) means to love them with all our desires — with everything that we cherish and value. Wherever our treasure is, there will be our heart. What fills our passions and appetites? If it is not God, then we are not loving God with all our heart. Jesus' heart is pierced on the cross to show us how much he loves us and longs in love to transform our hard and selfish hearts with his Sacred Heart. When we allow our own hearts to be pierced and emptied of false desires, then we can love others with the love of the heart of Jesus.

To love God with all our soul (cf. Mt 10:28; 11:29; 12:18; 26:38) is to love God with our truest, deepest self. It means to love God with our very character, our unique personality. To love God with our soul means to love him from our conscience — that is, to love him in the knowledge of our sinfulness and unworthiness. In other words, we love God with all our soul when we love him just the way we are, trusting that God's providence is at work even in our sinfulness. It is Jesus' soul that is filled with sorrow in Gethsemane. He allows himself to be stripped on Calvary so that we might see the full gift of his human soul that he lays down in love for us out of love for his Father. When we stand naked before God, not making excuses for any sin that we find in our soul, then we love God with all our soul.

To love Jesus with all our mind means to love him with our ability to reason. It means loving God with all our ideas, notions, opinions, conceptions, and convictions. But we love God with our mind only if all these things are one with the Truth who is Jesus Christ. Too often our lives become infested with attitudes, platitudes, philosophies, prejudices, and preconceptions that have nothing to do with the Gospel. We replace the Word of God with our own way of seeing things. To love God with our mind means to surrender to him the privatized way we prefer to understand and interpret things. It means to live only by the Truth who is Jesus. In his Passion, Jesus allows his head to be crowned with thorns to show us how much we must allow our own false ideas and judgments to be pierced and purified by the Blood of Christ. Then we let Jesus love us the way he wants to. And then we can love others with the love of Jesus.

Thirty-First Sunday in Ordinary Time

The Humble Exalted
Matthew 23:1-12

Before Christ, humility was not revered as a virtue but rather was reviled as something low and ignoble. According to the pagan mind, to cultivate humility was to accede to a life of servility. However, those who did not embrace humility were forced to rely on themselves in order to get ahead. In a certain respect, there was no logical way out of the pretentiousness that we see in the scribes and the Pharisees who lived for places of honor, prestige, accolades, and adulation. To be hidden and humble would only lessen their status as religious leaders.

But the revelation of Jesus Christ changes all that. The Gospel proclaims that humility is not a mark of weakness but rather a bona fide virtue that blesses the believer with distinct advantages. First of all, without Gospel humility we would remain trapped in our weaknesses, defects, and shortcomings, relying on hypocritical bravado in a futile attempt to survive. A poignant line from *The Imitation of Christ* reads, "If you seek yourself, you will find yourself — to your own ruin." However, the humility of the Gospel liberates us from the blackmail of the devil that seduces us into hiding our insecurity behind futile self-exaltation. In fact, the grace of Gospel humility fills us with the power to confront the truth about ourselves, in all our misery, full of confidence. When we are possessed with such humble hopefulness, God exalts us by blessing us with his goodness, which far exceeds all our failures.

Moreover, Gospel humility is habit-forming. The humility of Jesus is a way of life that keeps us on The Way. Humility is the principle of the life of faith. St. Thérèse of Lisieux attested, "I keep before me the image of myself as weak and imperfect, and in this I find my joy." The humility of Jesus saves us from pretending to be something that we are not. The humble, honest self-knowledge of our real nothingness becomes the indispensable means by which we welcome the uplifting love of the Father. Humility makes room for the kind of perfection only God can provide — a perfection that we cannot accomplish on our own, no matter how many titles and credentials the world may attribute to us. In the wonder of Christian humility, the more we realize how deficient we are, the more we rejoice in the knowledge of how gracious and generous God is.

Finally, once humility takes hold of us, our former self-serving ways get transformed into an eagerness to serve others. Only the revelation of Gospel humility assures us how much the real secret of happiness is not being selfish. Christian humility empowers us to renounce selfishness and to rechannel that energy with zeal to prosper the good of others. Ironically, authentic Christian greatness manifests itself in service, but in service assumed as the ultimate exaltation and not as a demotion.

Only with Gospel humility does the Eucharist make sense. If we, like the scribes and Pharisees, presume that ostentation and pomposity are the essence of worship, then the humility of the Host — elevated so that we may be exalted — remains for us a source of humiliation.

THIRTY-SECOND SUNDAY IN ORDINARY TIME

WISDOM, OIL, AND THE BRIDEGROOM
Matthew 25:1-13

According to the Fathers of the Church, the oil of today's parable symbolizes the virtue and interior illumination of those who have heard the Word of God and put it into practice (Mt 7:24). The oil is the holiness of their souls. St. Makarios of Egypt observed that we resemble the five foolish virgins when our hearts are not filled here and now with spiritual oil – the energy of the Spirit active in the virtues. He contends that the foolish virgins were held back by attachments and worldly affections that prevented them from offering the fullness of their love and longing to the celestial Bridegroom. This is because souls yearning after the sanctifying power of the Spirit not intrinsic to human nature direct all their love toward Christ, turning away from everything else. He concludes that people become "foolish virgins" when they opt to remain imprisoned in their own limited and impaired nature.

The foolishness of the five virgins resembles that of the foolish man who built his house on sandy ground – the foolishness of those who hear the Word of God but do not put it into practice (Mt 7:26). However, the other five virgins are wise because they capitalize on the absence of the bridegroom in order to cultivate a life of virtuousness that readies them for the wedding (Mt 9:15). Their virginity testifies to their innocence, and their prudence to their cleverness (Mt 10:16). They exemplify the faithful, farsighted servant Jesus has just described (Mt 24:45), one who knows how to dispense the provisions of the household at need. To the extent that they have heard the Word of God and put it into practice in a life of faith and purity, they resemble the only other virgin mentioned in the Gospel of Matthew: the virgin who conceives the Word and gives birth to the Bridegroom (Mt 1:23).

The reason why the wise virgins refuse to share their oil is simply that their oil cannot be shared. We cannot live others' lives for them. We cannot "lend" another our rectitude, our moral character. Personal holiness is unique and non-transferable. The only way to be able to meet the

Bridegroom is to become predisposed to meet him. This demands a life of sanctity, dedicated and devoted to the things of God, diligent and disciplined in all our desires and choices.

The door in the parable is closed and locked, but it is really the folly of the five — like the fraudulence of the scribes and Pharisees — that shuts the doors of God's kingdom on themselves (Mt 23:13). Scripturally, to be without oil signifies punishment for infidelity.

Oil is a source of light. The conscientiousness of the wise virgins regarding the oil reveals their desire to possess the ultimate source of light in their lives: Jesus Christ. The bridegroom welcomes the wise virgins into the wedding feast with him since, like the saints, they shine like the sun (Mt 13:43). Because the wise ones' lamps — that is, the uprightness of their lives — shine in a way that gives praise to the heavenly Father (Mt 5:15-16), they enjoy the feast of the Kingdom. In the Bible, oil symbolizes divine blessing. Moreover, abundance of oil is a sign of salvation. No wonder that oil plays such a crucial role in the Church's sacramental life: baptism, confirmation, holy orders, and anointing of the sick.

We want to be ready to greet Jesus the Bridegroom. We must, therefore, "stay awake" (cf. Mt 24:42-43). For in the darkness of night, heavy with slumber, it is not that the Bridegroom will pass us by. Rather, it is we who, in the Garden of Gethsemane, will act as if we do not know and love Jesus. Constant, heartfelt prayer keeps us solicitous and radiant with the oil of salvation. The Bridegroom sees himself in the wise virgins' light. And in their light, they see Light.

Thirty-Third Sunday in Ordinary Time

What the Talents Are Not
Matthew 25:14-30

This mystifying parable intrigues us to answer three crucial questions. First of all, who is the master? Unlike most high-ranking, aloof executives, this man not only knows his servants, but he possesses an intimate knowledge of their personal abilities right down to the most minute differences. Moreover, the master entrusts sizeable sums, not to brokers or bankers, but to mere servants. There is no indication that these three men are fiscal managers, unlike other specialized servants (Mt 13:52; 20:8; 24:45). What's more, the seeming foolishness of the action gets compounded when the master then goes away for a long time. For the funds held by the servants were sufficient for them to buy their way out of servitude, and the absence of the master gave them the ideal chance.

From all of this, we can conclude that the master is not out to multiply his fortune (otherwise he would have given all of the talents to the first servant). Nor does the master need to go away in order for the story to make sense. However, that clue signals that this parable is essentially about *trust*. By leaving them well-off and unsupervised, the master proffers the servants the opportunity to act in freedom. For the master's purpose is not to increase his assets, but to invite his servants to transformation. The master does not want to make more money; he wants his servants to make more of themselves united with him.

All of this is verified once the master returns. He does not even keep the newly gained income. Rather, all that the master desires is for the faithful ones to share his joy. To share another's joy signifies a harmonious union of wills founded on equality. The master's joy consists in seeing his servants transformed from slaves to sons as the fruit of their trust in the master.

So then, just who is the master? The key is found in the Greek verb used to describe the master's entrusting of his possessions: "hand over." Here again, Matthew does not use a word from the world of financial transactions, but rather the very expression that Jesus uses to describe his being handed over to crucifixion (cf. Mt 4:12; 5:25; 10:4, 17-21; 11:27; 17:22; 18:34; 20:18-19; 24:9, 10; 26:2, 15-25, 45-48; 27:2-4, 18, 26). In a way that no other word can, this verb expresses the fullest sense of what the sending and the giving of the Son means.

Therefore, the master is God the Father, and the talents are Jesus Christ himself — the Father's most precious "possession." Frequently, people confuse the talents for natural "talents," skills, gifts, or other personal capacities. But we must not confuse the master's talents with the servants' abilities. The abilities are the natural, earthly capabilities unique to each servant. The talents, however, are something beyond what they possess naturally, something extra entrusted to them by the master according to their abilities. The talents are the graces God supplies to our abilities in order to actualize, fulfill, and perfect them. The talents are not something natural but supernatural. God gives gifts commensurate to our own endowments so that grace might perfect nature.

Moreover, the talents belong to the *master*, not to the servants. It is the stewardship of the talents that transforms the servants from slavery to sonship. This parable is not about using our particular talents for the glory of God (Jesus has already preached that Good News — cf. Mt 5:13-16; Mt 10:8; etc.). For the talents generate more talents *just by being*. Rather, this parable, told to prepare us for Christ's imminent Passion, is about receiving the Father's gift of the Son and "capitalizing" on it in a way that honors the confidence and intention of the Father in entrusting Jesus to us according to our ability.

The parable is about accepting the Father's invitation to become perfect by investing to the full the sacred deposit of the Son in our life. The bestowal of the Father's treasure awakens us to real abilities that we never knew we had. United to the fortune of the Father, we can liquidate whatever enslaves us. God, who creates out of nothing, calls us to reap where we have not sown by fully "appreciating" the sacred collateral that we have been entrusted with.

Finally, who is the third servant? He claims that fear has prevented him from investing his talent, but the master sees him for what he is: a wicked, lazy servant. The greatest evil that the wicked servant commits is not trusting in the confidence which the master entrusts in him. To be "faithful in small matters" means using the graces of the life of Christ to deepen our relationship with the Master. The servant's distrust manifests a deep-seated pride that spurns the ready help which the first two servants could provide. Instead, he lets the gifts and abilities of the others paralyze and eclipse the significance of his own.

The wicked servant's rejection of the master's beneficence is tantamount to betrayal. And in burying the money, the parable reminds us of the one responsible for Jesus being buried in a tomb: Judas Iscariot. No wonder the master calls the third servant "useless" and consigns him to the worst kind of punishment in the Gospel (cf. Mt 8:12; 13:42, 50; 22:13; 24:51).

In short, this parable challenges us to believe in God's prerogative to make us partners in the process of justification, and to give full assent to it. The Master invests us, his servants, with what is precious to himself in order to elevate us and make us like himself. If we do not understand this parable correctly, we cannot understand the mystery of the cross.

CHRIST THE KING

Matthew 25:31-46

Those who unwittingly become "goats" upon the glorious return of the Son of Man as King do so through their failure to recognize Christ's startling majesty in the needy. As St. Teresa of Ávila expressed it: "O King of Glory and Lord of all kings! Upon beholding your person, one sees immediately that you alone, on account of the majesty you reveal, merit to be called Lord. To behold your majesty is startling; and the more one beholds along with this majesty, Lord, your humility and the love you show to someone like myself, the more startling it becomes."

Christ reveals his person in the person of others, especially the poor. Thus, to recognize Christ as King means to behold him in the person of our neighbor, to revere the Lord's humility, especially as it is reflected in the humility of the lowly, and to admit with profound gratitude our own unworthiness so as to receive his royal love.

Both the righteous and the punished ask, "Lord, when did we see you [in need]?" The sign that the righteous have truly "seen" Christ the King is the charitable service they have offered him in the person of those whose dignity was at stake. Conversely, the punished remain blind to Christ's kingship precisely because of their self-absorbed refusal to serve. For in the act of such service, we discover Jesus and the essence of Christ's kingship, which is service. Pope John Paul II has written that "the sharing in Christ's kingly mission, that is to say the fact of rediscovering in oneself and others the special dignity of our vocation, can be described as 'kingship.' This dignity is expressed in readiness to serve, in keeping with the example of Christ, who 'came not to be served but to serve.' If, in the light of this attitude of Christ's, 'being a king' is truly possible only by 'being a servant,' then 'being a servant' also demands so much spiritual maturity that it must really be described as 'being a king.' Our sharing in Christ's kingly mission – his 'kingly function' (*munus*) – is closely linked with every sphere of both Christian and human morality" (*Redemptor Hominis*, 21).

Second, to recognize Christ's kingship means to revere Jesus' own

134

humility that elevates the human condition of humility to that of virtue. As a result, to be subject to Christ the King is not to be "put upon" but rather "taken out" of our false self. To live the kingdom of God entails much more than mere moral conformity to law. To live the kingdom of God means remaining humbly submissive and obedient to the movement of Jesus Christ. We revere Christ's humility by rejecting all self-dependence and by uniting ourselves to the virtue of Christ that lessens in us the remnants of sin, thereby increasing our desire and ability to do good to others. Jesus is the King when he saves us by his death. Humbly entering into that saving death by dying to self is the principal act of Kingdom living.

Finally, the hungry, thirsty, homeless, naked, ill, and imprisoned are seemingly those least deserving of the loving attention of a king. That is why Christ the King seeks them out first in a preferential way. Only thankfulness saves us from the presumption that would lead us to forget our own unworthiness and to take for granted the care of Christ the King. Therefore, we honor Christ as King by keeping the will of God foremost in all our thoughts, motives, decisions, desires, words, and actions. Then we cannot help but call Jesus Christ Lord and King, for then we behold the sovereignty of Christ the King in our own person, in the person of our neighbor, and in the Body of Christ. And then, in a very real way, Christ's startling majesty becomes mystically our own.

PART TWO:
REFLECTIONS ON SOLEMNITIES AND ALSO FEASTS THAT MAY FALL ON SUNDAY

THE IMMACULATE CONCEPTION

SUBLIME CREDIT TO OUR RACE
Luke 1:26-38

At the time of this writing, there is a lottery ticket worth two million dollars floating around somewhere in New Jersey. If it is not claimed before December 10, the ticket will become invalid — a worthless scrap of paper. Such nonchalance about something so precious seems beyond human comprehension. How can someone possess a thing so priceless and life-changing and yet be so indifferent and negligent toward it?

The mystery of the Immaculate Conception of the Blessed Virgin Mary is much like that astounding lottery ticket. How ironic it is that this occurrence falls so close to the solemnity of the Immaculate Conception. For, in the Immaculate Conception of the Blessed Virgin Mary, God the Father has blessed his people with an unfathomable wealth of riches. That tiny person in the womb of St. Anne, destined to become the Mother of God, possesses in her very being the fullness of divine favor that exceeds all our longings and imagining. Like that lottery ticket, all God asks on this glorious feast is that we claim the grace that comes to us in Mary, not because of our good fortune, but because of the unimaginable immensity of the Father's initiative, providence, and compassion.

Such divine generosity would remain inconceivable on our part if God himself did not cause Mary to be conceived immaculately in the womb of her mother. Mary's Immaculate Conception is the ticket! Although before her birth — like that misplaced lottery ticket — the inestimable value of Mary's presence in our life remains unseen, it nonetheless alerts us to how radically impoverished and wanting we really are. The Immaculate Conception, like that lottery ticket, signals a chance for a revolutionary new beginning in our life — the chance to leave behind everything about us that is worn out, wretched, weak, feeble, and crippling. With the heavenly principal that comes to us in the Immaculate Conception, we can throw out what is old and make a clean break with what is brand new. The mystery of the Immaculate Conception is the lottery chance that God takes in offering us innocence anew.

Not long ago, someone stole my credit card and went on a twenty-four-hour spending spree to the tune of four thousand dollars before I discovered that the card was missing and canceled it. In the Immaculate Conception, God manifests his marvelous, mind-boggling justice in a similar way. He puts into our hands something that is not ours by right, something that we do not deserve — namely, the immaculate purity, integrity, and goodness of the Blessed Virgin Mary — and he commands us to capitalize on it to the max. God wants us to "take advantage" of the once-in-a-lifetime opportunity the Immaculate Conception affords.

We don't own our credit cards; they belong to the credit card company. But in our hand, how a credit card can transform our life. The gift of Mary Immaculate today is God's solemn invitation to that incomparable transformation. We will never become the Immaculate Conception. But united to the Blessed Virgin Mary as her devoted, loving children, all the rich, resplendent graces of her life that she owns from the moment of her Immaculate Conception become our own. We become Mary's.

CHRISTMAS

HOW THE BIRTH OF JESUS COMES ABOUT
Matthew 1:1-25

The first Christmas-that-almost-wasn't story concerns good St. Joseph. This righteous man, for selfless and noble reasons, decided to divorce his wife, Mary. But an angel of God intervened to bless Joseph with assurance about the workings of Providence and to inform his judgment to act in a godly, redemptive manner. What the angel speaks to the future patron of the Church he speaks also to our heart so that we will fully embrace the mystery of the Incarnation and live out of its meaning as Emmanuel comes into our life.

First of all, the angel instructs Joseph not to be afraid to take Mary into his home. The same heavenly counsel remains crucial to our sanctifying experience of Christmas. The Mozarabic liturgy for Christmas beseeches God in these words:

> We beg you to renew your birth in human nature, penetrating us with your invisible godhead as you did in a unique way in Mary and do now spiritually in the Church. May you be conceived by our faith, that a mind untouched by corruption may bring you forth, that the soul, ever confirmed by the power of the Most High, may offer you a dwelling place.

The angel instructs us to take Mary into our homes so that, through the Incarnation, our souls may become worthy dwelling places of the Son of God.

Moreover, the angel enlightens Joseph to the saving truth that Mary has conceived through the Holy Spirit. Impaired human nature is naturally suspicious, skeptical, defensive, and prone to jump to the wrong conclusions. We require a supernatural intervention — a divine "conception" — in our own lives as well, in order to transform all our twisted and distorted conceptions. The theologian Hans Urs von Balthasar once wrote

141

that "man's alienation from God has so buried in oblivion so many of man's own deepest aspects that these can be brought up again into the light of memory and human self-understanding only through God's Incarnation." By welcoming the unfathomable truth that the angel reveals to Joseph and to us, the Holy Spirit purifies our memory and self-understanding, and perfects the divine likeness within us so that man's deepest aspects, fully alive, can become the very glory of God.

And finally, the angel instructs Joseph to give the child the name Jesus. We, too, are commanded over and over again to say the Name of Jesus, for in that sacred naming we realize the salvation from our sins. Without the Name of Jesus, sin continues its stranglehold on humanity, and we foolishly disregard the eternal salvation offered in the mortal flesh of a tiny infant. The Catholic novelist Sigrid Undset once wrote:

> When we give each other Christmas gifts in his Name, let us remember that he has given us the sun and the moon and the stars, and the earth with its forests and mountains and oceans — and all that lives and moves upon them. He has given us all green things and everything that blossoms and bears fruit — and all that we quarrel about and all that we have misused — and to save us from our own foolishness, from all our sins, he came down to earth and gave us himself.

Let us awake like St. Joseph and do as God's messenger commands us. Our fitting response is articulated in a prayer from the Syriac Christmas liturgy:

> Make us worthy, Lord, to celebrate and to conclude in peace the feast which magnifies the rising of your light, by avoiding empty words, working with justice, fleeing from the passions, and raising up the spirit above earthly goods.

Mary, Mother of God

Led to the Mother
Luke 2:16-21

There is a stunning line in Pope John Paul II's beautiful little book *Gift and Mystery*. In reflecting on his youth, the Holy Father writes, "I was already convinced that *Mary leads us to Christ*, but at that time I began to realize also that *Christ leads us to his mother*." We see this dynamic at work in today's Gospel. After the angel appears to the shepherds and announces the birth of Jesus Christ to them, the shepherds leave their fields and go in haste to Bethlehem where they find, not just the Christ child, but also Mary (and Joseph). Their search for God's Son leads them to the Mother of God.

The solemnity of the Mother of God reminds us that Christ leads us to Mary so that we will constantly live in her. For it is through our union with the Mother of God that we receive the fullness of the life of Christ.

In reflecting on the Great Jubilee 2000, Pope John Paul II wrote, "Veneration of the Blessed Virgin Mary, when properly understood, can in no way take away from the dignity and efficacy of Christ the one Mediator." In particular, the Holy Father singles out the importance of St. Louis de Montfort's classic Marian treatise, *True Devotion to the Blessed Virgin*, by stating that "the essential theological truths which it contains are undeniable."

In that book, St. Louis de Montfort asks, "Is our purity sufficiently great to warrant our uniting ourselves with our Lord, directly and of ourselves?" The saint answers in the negative by asserting, "I do not believe that any person can achieve intimate union with our Lord and perfect fidelity to the Holy Spirit unless he has established a very deep union with the Blessed Virgin and a great dependence on her help."

Mary's maternal mediation does not end at Christmas. The Nativity is only a beginning. For, in the words of Montfort, "God the Son desires to be formed and, as it were, to be incarnated daily in his members through his mother. God the Son is daily formed and engendered only through the Most Blessed Virgin, in union with the Holy Spirit; and only through her does he communicate his merits and his virtues." St. Maximilian Kolbe echoes this: "As the first-born God-man and not otherwise, all souls in Christ, through the love of God for and in the Immaculate One, are reborn. And no word takes flesh, no perfection or virtue is incarnated or realized in anyone, but through the love of God for the Immaculate One."

The Holy Father exclaims, "Yes, Mary does bring us closer to Christ; she does lead us to him, provided that we live her mystery in Christ." Montfort sums it all up: "Whoever finds Mary shall find life – that is, shall find Jesus Christ, who is the Way, the Truth, and the Life."

As we begin this new year, the Church blesses us anew with the maternal mediation of the Mother of God so that we can live the Blessed Virgin Mary's mystery in Christ. In that way, the life of Christ will come to full fruition in us.

The Presentation of the Lord

The Presentation and the Assumption
Luke 2:22-40

The dramatic apse mosaic of the Basilica of St. Mary Major in Rome illustrates the life of the Blessed Virgin Mary. The great centerpiece of the mosaic depicts Christ in the act of crowning his mother Queen of Heaven. However, just below that image one sees a moving scene of the dormition of Mary. The body of the Blessed Virgin lies on a bier surrounded by angels and the apostles. Jesus stands behind the body of his mother. In his arms, Jesus holds what looks like a little child wrapped in swaddling clothes. In fact, the infant figure represents the soul of the Mother of God, whom the Son of God is carrying to heaven. Thus, in a strange and wonderful way, the artist portrays the Assumption of the Blessed Virgin Mary as the converse to the Presentation of the Lord.

The shared elements of both scenes indicate the core traits of these two great mysteries of the faith. In both episodes, the subject presented to God is a child. In both, the offering is made via the arms of God's holy one. And in both, the infant is consecrated to God in a kind of homecoming.

The Presentation commemorates the revelation of the light of Christ's glory, by which we gain a first glimpse of the heavenly salvation that awaits us. And the Assumption celebrates Mary's personal entrance into that eternal splendor, as the reward for her perfect conformity to her Son — in effect, the consummation of the mystery of the Presentation.

It is fitting for Jesus to be presented to his Father as a child because the kingdom of God belongs to little children (Lk 18:16). Today it is the Father who silently beckons, "Let the little children come to me," referring to his own incarnate Son. Only the one who accepts the kingdom of God as a child will enter into it (Lk 18:17). Jesus exemplifies this truth today, as does the depiction of Mary in the St. Mary Major mosaic.

Christ will soon teach, "Whoever receives this child in my name receives me, and whoever receives me receives the one who sent me" (Lk

9:48). Thus, the Presentation offers Simeon and Anna a concrete occasion to welcome Jesus and his Father. At the same time, the Presentation affords us the graced opportunity to welcome spiritual childhood in our own lives of faith. By that welcome, we will know how much the Father welcomes us into the embrace of his love and longs for us to be one with him in heaven.

Simeon takes the child Jesus into his arms and blesses God. Mary proclaims in her Magnificat, "[God's] mercy is from age to age / to those who fear him. / He has shown might with his arm" (Lk 1:50-51). The Father manifests his might in the way that he wields divine mercy to confound and depose the wiles of the world. Jesus relies on the physical arms of Mary and Joseph to accomplish his presentation in the temple; he cannot do it alone. In the same way, all Christians must surrender themselves to the might of God in the manner he deigns to unfold it: by being folded in the protection of his arms. Without such personal communion with the Three-Personed God, heaven cannot make sense to us.

Finally, Jerusalem symbolizes our final home of heaven (Heb 12:22; Gal 4:24-31). There is no temple in the heavenly Jerusalem because the Lord himself is its temple, and the glory of the lamp of the Lamb of God gives it light (Rv 21:23). From the first moments of his life, Jesus is making his way to his glorious death in Jerusalem. As a result, the Presentation calls us to spend our life living fully for God, the whole of our body and soul devoted to the will of the Father. The presentation of our complete gift of self out of love leads us in faith to the hope-filled assumption of eternal life.

St. Joseph, Husband of Mary

The Mission of Joseph
Luke 2:41-51a

This episode of the finding in the temple reveals as much about the foster-father of the Son of God as it does about Jesus himself. For this event further galvanizes Joseph's God-given personal mission to be the husband of Mary.

Hans Urs von Balthasar wrote, "It is when God addresses a conscious subject, tells him who he is and what he means to the eternal God of truth, and shows him the purpose of his existence – that is, imparts a distinctive and divinely authorized mission – that we can say of a conscious subject that he is a 'person.' " In a dream (Mt 1:20-21), God addresses Joseph and tells him what he means to the eternal God: he is to be an earthly father to the incarnate Truth. Joseph fulfills the purpose of his existence by loving Mary with the love of a supremely devoted husband. As Von Balthasar commented, when Mary marries Joseph, "God's intervention does not dissolve this marriage but simultaneously uses and transcends it."

From the instant of that famous dream, Joseph realizes that he will become the person God destines him to be only in Mary and Jesus. In the midst of the experience of being without the physical presence of Jesus for the first time, Joseph's love for Mary deepens as he shares her sorrow. Joseph's search for his Son is at once a search to know God's will, to be in communion with his destiny, and to be an effective instrument of Providence. He accomplishes this through his union with Mary.

Ecclesiastical writer Jacob of Serug explained:

> Joseph did not look on the blessed one as a man on his wife; he looked on her as the high priest looks on the Holy of Holies. He was loving her and marveling at her and bowing to her; he was honoring her and reverencing her and serving her. He was regarding her like the cloud over Mount Sinai, because within her the Power of the Godhead

was dwelling. His heart was pure, and also his thoughts were holy; he bows and gives thanks because he was deemed worthy to be a priest to the Son.

In the experience of the lost Son, Joseph begins to realize his vocation to be the Patron of the Church. He finds his truest self in Jesus through Mary when he finds Jesus with Mary.

In this way, Joseph is like all of us: we come to Jesus through Mary. When at last Joseph and Mary find their Son in the temple, it is Mary, and not the father, who speaks to their wayward boy. The mother's words voice how forsaken the foster-father feels by the Son, rendering supernatural meaning to this otherwise incomprehensible mystery. As Joseph listens – and as we listen – to Mary address her Son, he comes to understand how Jesus' whole mission is about being in his Father's house, about his Father's business. One day in the future, once again in Jerusalem, the Son on the cross will feel forsaken by the heavenly Father. But, as the finding in the temple after three days of being lost foreshadows, the feeling of being forsaken leads to the most intimate union with God. The silent husband of Mary images the way that we are to approach the Lord in worship, united with the Mother of God and attentive to her words, in order to become the persons God destines us to become.

All of this causes St. Ephrem the Syrian to sing:

> Joseph rose to serve in the presence of his Lord who was within Mary. The priest serves in the presence of your Ark because of your holiness. Moses bore the tablet of stone that his Lord had written. And Joseph escorted the pure tablet in whom was dwelling the Son of the Creator. The tablets were left behind since the world was filled with your teaching.

Joseph shows us how to find that sacred teaching.

THE ANNUNCIATION OF THE LORD

ABOLISHING THE CONFLICT
Luke 1:26-38

In the fullness of time, God sent forth to the world his own Son born of a woman. What is it that makes the time of the Annunciation "full"?

For one thing, obviously, the Blessed Virgin Mary had biologically entered into her childbearing years. But more than that, despite her personal sinlessness, Mary must have had enough life experience by this time to witness the reality of sin in the world. Moreover, the Blessed Virgin's consciousness of sin must have distressed her Immaculate Heart. The anguish at seeing the effects of sin surely troubled Mary's soul. Otherwise, Mary would have possessed no awareness of the world's need for a Savior, which would have rendered Gabriel's announcement meaningless. It is said that St. Dominic would often spend the entire night in church, deep in prayer, weeping as he pleaded, "O Lord, what will become of sinners?" Perhaps that was how Mary prayed as well until the arrival of Gabriel. St. Bernard confirms this when he writes, "If you, my Lady, let him hear your voice, then he will let you see our salvation. Isn't this what you have been wanting, what you have been weeping for and sighing after, day and night, in your prayers?"

We are told that Mary was greatly troubled and that she pondered the meaning of the angel's greeting. Clearly, this encounter between a woman and an angel recalls Eve's fateful exchange with an evil angel in Eden. There Eve gave her consent to the sin that proceeded in its effect to defile all of humanity. Eve conceded to iniquity because, in listening to Satan, she let herself be deceived. So eager was she to be like God that she foolishly forfeited her relationship of love with him. However, the prudent Mary is not over-quick to trust the message of an angel. Thus, Gabriel has to prove his credibility. He does so by revealing that he knows the pristine state of Mary's soul: "Hail, full of grace!" Only Mary herself in her humility could know the reality of her immaculate condition — of the absolute absence of sin in her life. And only a holy angel would rejoice in it. At this moment, the angel's acknowledgement of Mary's Immaculate Conception confirms that Gabriel is the real thing.

However, having accepted the messenger, Mary still needs to deal with the weightiness of the message. Jacob of Serug wrote that, at the Annunciation, "a pure virgin and a fiery Watcher met each other and conversed in argument" about "that great strife which occurred amidst the trees." They "spoke with wonder on the matter until they abolished the conflict between the Lord and Adam" — a "discourse which reconciled dwellers of earth and heaven." Then "the struggle between the two sides ceased, and there was peace."

At peace with the messenger and the message, the Holy Virgin now only seeks clarity about the means: "The power of the Most High will overshadow you." In other words, the Incarnation is the fruit of the Blessed Virgin Mary agreeing to live by a love that exceeds the love of family, friendship, or even marriage. In the same way, for us the Annunciation is about letting God love us with his consummate love that surpasses the imagining and the fantasy of the world. Only that love saves us from death-dealing deception and gives us divine peace.

The grace of the Annunciation becomes our own when we pray like St. Ildephonsus of Toledo, in the seventh century:

> Holy Virgin, I beg you: enable me to receive Jesus from the Spirit, according to the same process by which you bore Jesus. May my soul possess Jesus thanks to the Spirit through whom you conceived Jesus. May the grace to know Jesus be granted to me through the Spirit who enabled you to know how to possess Jesus and bring him forth.

THE ASCENSION OF THE LORD

MEMORY, WORD, PRESENCE
Matthew 28:16-20

How remarkable it is that even at this late date the eleven disciples still "doubted." What more than the Resurrection do the apostles of Jesus Christ need to eradicate the doubt that lingers in their hearts? God knows. That is why the Lord orders them to meet him on "the mountain." The mountain is where Jesus experienced temptation (Mt 4:8) and preached the Beatitudes (Mt 5:1). The mountain is the place where faith is tried and faith is strengthened. Those possessed of a profound faith can in fact move mountains with it (Mt 17:20; 21:21). Jesus thus approaches the Eleven on the mountain to perfect their faith, which will receive its test the moment that Jesus ascends out of view.

Without the ascension of Jesus, the disciples' faith might never be quickened. As long as Christ can be seen with the eyes, reliance on faith takes a back seat. But the risen Jesus commands his disciples to "make disciples of all nations . . . teaching them to observe all that I have commanded you." Only when Christ himself cannot be bodily observed does his corpus of teaching come to the fore through the operation of the disciples' memory. Holy dependence on memory purifies our faith, deepens insight into the truth, clarifies confusion, filters out distractions, and integrates thought and understanding. For, as Msgr. Luigi Giussani observes, "Memory is the awareness of a Presence." Through the dynamic of memory, the teaching of Jesus acts as a light on the path of faith, illuminating our own progress to heaven and making it secure.

Christians take up this commission with confidence. For, although Jesus ascends to the right hand of his Father, the saving events of the Paschal Mystery never end. Their salutary power continues to be active unceasingly in the world, redeeming those who submit to their force. However, Christ's saving events reach us now, not through the pre-Calvary bodily touch of Jesus, but rather via the living Word of God: Sacred Scripture. St. Peter of Damascus wrote:

You have ascended with Christ into the transcendent world through the knowledge of intelligible realities and of the mysteries hidden in the divine Scriptures. You move from fear to religious devotion, from which springs spiritual knowledge; from this knowledge comes judgment, that is, discrimination; from discrimination comes the strength that leads to understanding; from thence you come to wisdom.

The all-encompassing power that has been given to Christ gets imparted to apostles set apart to reveal the mysteries hidden in Sacred Scripture. The Word proclaimed activates the life-giving energy of the ending events of Christ's earthly ministry. Thanks to the apostles' ministry — the ministry of the Church — all believers ascend with Christ into the heaven of wisdom.

In this way, the mystery of the Ascension poses us with the challenge to be resolute. We are lost if we live only by what can be empirically known. We are misled if we dismiss Sacred Scripture as merely a textbook or a manual of maxims. Even more, we are doomed if we interpret Christ's ascent into heaven as a departure that leaves absence in its wake. Jesus assures us, "I am with you always, until the end of the age." Perhaps it is only with the Ascension that we really come to believe the efficacy of Christ's Real Presence in the Holy Eucharist. Jesus commands his Church to baptize the nations in the name of the Blessed Trinity. By existentially sharing in Christ's death and Resurrection, we come to behold his salvific presence in every aspect of existence — a sight that elevates us to be one with Our Lord.

THE NATIVITY OF ST. JOHN THE BAPTIST

HERALD OF THE SACRAMENTS
Luke 1:57-66, 80

To celebrate the nativity of John the Baptist is to anticipate the "birth" of the sacraments instituted by Jesus Christ. John is forever identified with the sacrament that is the gateway to life in the Spirit and the basis of the whole Christian life: baptism. John's own "baptism" occurs in the womb of his mother, Elizabeth, at the visitation of the Mother of God. His configuration to Jesus Christ is signified by his leaping in the womb (Lk 1:41). After disappearing into the desert to grow up and mature in spirit (Lk 1:80), John appeared in the region of the Jordan preaching reform of life and baptizing all those who came to him.

However, even after receiving John's baptism, the people seek a way to be more perfectly bound to the good news that John animates in them. Without understanding it, they yearn for the special strength of the Holy Spirit that enriches and informs their lives. In this way, John's proclamation that the Messiah "will baptize you with the Holy Spirit and fire" (Mt 3:11; Lk 3:16) prefigures the Sacrament of Confirmation.

The Eucharist is the sacrament whereby Christ associates his followers with the sacrifice that he himself offered on the cross. In his prison cell, John the Baptist remains confident that Jesus is the Real Presence of the Messiah. For the report that Jesus sends back to John's messengers (Lk 7:22-23) testifies to the Eucharistic effects of Christ's actions in the world. So convicted is he about Christ's incarnate presence that John allows himself to be sacrificed in beheading rather than compromise his communion with Jesus Christ.

The whole of John the Baptist's life was marked by penance (e.g., Lk 5:33). On the day of his naming, John's father, Zechariah, declares, "You will go before the Lord to prepare his ways, / to give his people knowledge of salvation / through the forgiveness of their sins" (Lk 1:76-77). The refusal on the part of the high priests and Pharisees to confess the truth about John's identity prevents them from sharing in the reconciliation offered by Jesus Christ (Lk 20:1-8).

John "preached the good news to the people" (Lk 3:18). The preaching of John presages the priesthood of the Church. The Sacrament of Holy Orders was instituted to proclaim the Word of God and to restore communion with God by sacrifices and prayers. Significantly, John's priestlike example becomes the impetus for Jesus to teach his disciples the Lord's Prayer: "Lord, teach us to pray just as John taught his disciples" (Lk 11:1).

Although John the Baptist was never married, his selfless devotion to the Other — "I am not worthy to loosen the thongs of his sandals" (Lk 3:16) — remains a prime model for the sanctifying power of marriage. For, as the *Catechism* teaches, "marriage helps to overcome self-absorption, egoism, pursuit of one's own pleasure, and to open oneself to the other, to mutual aid and to self-giving" (1609).

And finally, the Sacrament of Anointing of the Sick completes our conformity to the death and Resurrection of Christ. The martyrdom of John testifies how much Christian death is not an ending but rather a real beginning. Even in his death, the witness of John continues to be an instrument of redemption. Thanks to the profundity of John's faith, people see beyond the constraints of death and presume that he has been raised from the dead (Lk 9:7-8). Even the apostles assess the stunning power of Jesus by the greatness of John (Lk 9:19).

Jesus confesses that there is no man born of woman greater than John (Lk 7:28). Yet, the least born into the kingdom of God is greater than John. The sacraments make that birth into the Kingdom possible, and John the Baptist heralds them in his holy life.

Sts. Peter and Paul, Apostles

Belonging and Apostleship
Matthew 16:13-19

Msgr. Luigi Giussani has written that "whoever withdraws from belonging to God is estranged from everyone. He's alone, defined moreover by economic and commercial parameters; he lives another, apparent belonging that does not exist, that is the only position for denying belonging to God. You cannot speak of belonging to God without grasping, following, and imitating all that he has decided to make man know."

Both St. Peter and St. Paul experienced such withdrawal from belonging to God at poignant moments in their lives. Peter brought it on himself when he denied Jesus three times, and Paul incited withdrawal in his persecution of Christians. Both actions resulted in estrangement, and out of that mutual experience of estrangement rose the greatness of these two apostles.

The fact is that Jesus never ceases to pose the question, "Who do people say that the Son of Man is?" And he relies on the witness of his apostles to lead the withdrawn and estranged into the saving embrace of God. For Sts. Peter and Paul are blessed with a preeminent capacity for grasping, following, and imitating all that the Lord has decided for men and women to know. Their intimate knowledge and understanding of God is the fruit of throwing off all the denial about God that once polluted their lives. In them, "apparent belonging" has been transformed into unbounded belonging to and for God.

It is so easy for us to get caught up in a kind of daily dualism that creates a tension between our faith and the "economic and commercial parameters" that we live by. When Peter replied to Jesus' question by saying, "You are the Christ, the Son of the living God," his answer implied that from that moment on there could be no dualism in his life. Jesus was to be *his* Christ; life means living deeply united to the Son of the living God. To seek meaning, purpose, or fulfillment outside of that revelation is to withdraw from the belonging that Jesus desires of each of us.

We celebrate the two great apostles today in order to know how to identify and root out all the "apparent belonging" in our own lives so that we will live fully for God, imbued with the very life of Christ. Jesus longs for us to grasp, follow, and imitate all that he enabled us to know in his incarnation, and we do that through the witness, the prayers, and the protection of the great apostles Peter and Paul.

The medieval work *The Golden Legend* relates a story about Theophilus imprisoning St. Peter because he objects to Peter's preaching of the Gospel. When St. Paul learns of Peter's imprisonment, he visits Peter secretly in his cell. There Paul finds Peter weakened almost to the point of death. Paul weeps and cries out, "O my brother Peter, my glory, my joy, the half of my soul, now that I am here you must recover your strength!" With that, Peter opens his eyes and recognizes Paul, and Paul feeds his brother apostle so that Peter's strength returns. Then, together, they proceed to convert Theophilus to the faith.

May we find in the holy apostles Peter and Paul our glory, our joy, and the nourishment our souls require to leave behind all withdrawal, estrangement, and dualism in order to belong wholly to God.

THE TRANSFIGURATION OF THE LORD

TRANSFIGURATION AND VIRTUE
Matthew 17:1-9

The Transfiguration reveals to us what we are destined to become in Jesus Christ. Whereas Christ's transfiguration is sudden and spectacular, ours is often gradual and unremarkable.

One of the chief things that distinguishes us from the angels is that they, from the first moment of their creation, are complete and fully realized beings. We, on the other hand, live in a state of constant becoming. To be human is to be a creature blessed with a potential that we progressively actualize through the graced use of freedom. Christ's transfiguration shows us just how perfect we can become by remaining united to him.

To say that our transfiguration relies on the proper use of the gift of freedom is to speak of the dynamic of virtue. Virtue is a habitual and firm disposition to do good. Such a disposition signifies openness to a creative activity, like the openness of Peter before the breathtaking spectacle of the Transfiguration. The glory that we witness in the Transfiguration is the result of the human nature of Jesus being united to the divine Second Person of the Blessed Trinity. Although the manner is different, our personal transfiguration is also the fruit of uniting the fullness of our human lives to the Person of Jesus Christ, relying on his divine power to transform us.

Virtue is not a figment of the imagination; it is real and realizable, shaping our whole body and soul. When we use our free will to make choices that configure us radically to Jesus Christ, then our emotional life becomes utterly rectified. Virtue works by impressing Gospel-formed reason on all the unruly and rebellious lower powers of our soul. In virtue, we discover the divine design that orders all our appetites to that holier, higher way of living signified by the "high mountain" of the Transfiguration. The more we surrender ourselves to the Gospel as the supreme norm for life, the more virtue effects in us the truth of life: the radiant reflection of God's Eternal Law, as resplendent in us as was Christ's appearance on the mountain.

When we are quickened by virtue, then we see "no one else but Jesus alone" in all the actions, imaginings, thoughts, and events that we encounter in life. Virtuous people tend toward the good with all their sensory and spiritual powers. Just as we witness both Christ's humanity and divinity at once in the Transfiguration, so too through the efficacy of virtue do we recognize the union of the human and the godly at work in us. From the moment of the creation of the first man and woman, human beings are destined to be fully divinized by God in glory. Through our participating in the sanctifying power of the Holy Spirit, as St. Athanasius remarks, "we become communicants in the divine nature. . . . For this reason, those in whom the Spirit dwells are divinized."

Thus, to become transfigured like Christ entails integrating our reason with the mind of Christ. We know from daily experience just how much the intentions and motives that fill our mind affect how we use our body. The way we think actually determines how our body works. For what occupies our mind invariably appears in our body language. That is why Christ's transfiguration does not take the form of an "idea." Rather, Jesus appears to us in the luminescence of his body to get us to change the way we think so that our minds will become radically conformed to the Gospel. In turn, the effect of our openness to the Lord's creative action emerges in the rectitude of *our* body and soul.

In short, the Transfiguration is about reconvicting us regarding the wonder of sanctity. As St. Gregory of Nyssa sums it up, "Ideas create idols; only wonder leads to knowing."

THE ASSUMPTION

TRANSLATION TO LIFE
Luke 1:39-56

The dynamic central to the Visitation helps us to understand the great mystery of the Assumption of the Blessed Virgin Mary. In the Visitation Gospel account, we read how Mary's presence in the house of Zechariah transforms the life of John the Baptist in the womb of his mother, Elizabeth.

At such an early stage of life, one would think that the only person capable of direct, life-changing contact with an unborn child would be the baby's own mother. Yet if Mary's presence is that powerful in "a town of Judah," how much more efficacious is the Blessed Mother's presence in heaven for those of us who await "a new birth to a living hope through the resurrection of Jesus Christ" (1 Pt 1:3).

Another name for the Assumption of Mary is the "translation," as a prayer from the Eastern liturgy celebrates: "In falling asleep, you did not forsake the world, O Theotokos! You were translated to life, O Mother of Life, and by your prayers you deliver our souls from death!" In a wonderful way, the celestial translation of the Mother of God helps us to "translate" our own lives that too often perplex us like a foreign language. Mary's assumption radiates the ultimate meaning and purpose of our own lives, and gives us a rectified way of interpreting the events of our lives.

The key rests in the fact that God does not will for Mary's body to rest on earth. For there is an intricate, essential connection between soul and body. As Dom Aelred Graham has written, "The soul is the rightful master of the body; the body is within the soul — not indeed spatially, but in virtue of its relation to it as an instrument." The Lord assumes the Blessed Virgin Mary's body into heaven because it is the perfect instrument of Mary's immaculate soul.

This truth helps us to grasp the conviction of a stunning insight of St. Thomas Aquinas: "The grace of a single soul is a greater thing than the natural good of the whole universe." In the beauty of the assumed body and soul of the Mother of God is contained the fullness of the beauty of the whole universe. The more we reflect in faith upon the mystery of the Assumption, the more we come to recognize the consummate grace of our own soul and of the souls of others. As C. S. Lewis put it: "It is with awe . . . that we should conduct all our dealings with one another, all friendships, all loves, all play, all politics. There are no *ordinary* people. You have never talked to a mere mortal."

The challenge of the Assumption is to abolish any dualism that we create between body and soul. We do so by imploring the maternal mediation of Mary to make our soul the rightful master of our body so that our body glorifies God as a holy instrument of our soul. That integrity of life is the fruit of our communion in the Church. And, as Fr. Benedict Ashley, O.P., observes, in the doctrine of Mary's Assumption "we can conceive the Church as the Body of Christ in every stage of completion from baptism to glory in a continuous process of resurrection to new life." Mary's assumption translates all the seeming insignificance of our life so that we can appreciate God's providence at work moment by moment, and so that we can be translated with her from glory to glory.

THE EXALTATION OF THE HOLY CROSS

HOW TO EXALT THE HOLY CROSS
John 3:13-17

How many of us spend much of our time doing everything in our power to avoid the cross. We readily, erroneously equate the cross with trouble, pain, conflict, and burden — or, at the very least, inconvenience. The world sees the cross as getting in the way of getting ahead. Nowadays high-powered physical exams exist for wannabe executives that forecast whether some catastrophic illness lies in store for the potential employee sometime in the future. That specter of the cross can and does dissuade certain employers from hiring perfectly qualified candidates.

The cross of Jesus Christ is not to be evaded but exalted. Yet, how do we exalt the cross?

First of all, we exalt the cross by not dreading it. In a moving prayer, St. Anselm addresses the cross as if it were a person. He says, "We do not acknowledge you because of the cruelty that godless and foolish men prepared you to effect upon the most gentle Lord, but because of the wisdom and goodness of him who of his own free will took you up."

We testify to that wisdom and goodness when we exalt the cross by hanging a crucifix on our wall in an act of faith. Then as we approach the cross of Christ united to his wisdom and goodness, the harshness of the cross gives way to the graciousness of God that predominates.

Advertising moguls know only too well how readily we, lying relaxed and serenely on the beach in the summertime, will look up to view a low-flying airplane passing ahead. That is why they attach so many annoying advertisements to the plane's tail. Jesus must be "lifted up" so that we will take our eyes off our mundane miseries and preoccupations, and place them on the only thing that makes any real difference in our life — the cross of Jesus Christ.

Second, we exalt the cross by embracing the hope that it proclaims. St. Theodore the Studite points out that "with the cross we are freed from the restraint of the enemy and we clutch on to the strength of salvation. The cross draws out praise from the angels and confuses demons."

161

In other words, when we take up the cross, the devil sees not our weakness but the towering strength of Jesus Christ crucified. That living image of Christ crucified confounds the devil and sends him fleeing. This is why we exalt the cross by blessing ourselves with the sign of the cross. The key for us, then, lies in claiming the cross with the hope of the angels and not the horror of the devils. For when we clutch on to the source of salvation with the trust of that supernatural hope, angels exult at the way we exalt the cross.

And third, we exalt the cross through the life of love that the holy cross empowers us to live. St. Catherine of Siena teaches us that "we cannot produce or give any other fruit but the fruit we have taken from the tree of life." The cross is not the intersection of two slabs of lifeless lumber. Rather, it remains a living, life-giving tree that calls us to be ever conjoined to it, like the vine and the branches. St. Leo the Great writes that "there was no other reason for the Son of God to be born than that he might be fixed to a cross."

The fruit of charity is possible in our life only through our communion with that fertile tree — a communion that first requires our total self-giving to this mystery. Yet, such self-abandonment is not a burden but a consolation. That is what our kiss at the veneration of the cross on Good Friday signifies. As St. Catherine counsels us, "Always find your rest in the branches of the true tree." Then we can join St. Anselm in praying, "Though now I serve God between hope and fear, I am sure that if I give thanks, love, and live to your glory, through you I shall at last come to that good."

ALL SAINTS

HOW TO TELL IF SOMEONE IS HOLY
Matthew 5:1-12a

One of the greatest glories of the Church is the privilege of declaring certain of her members "saints." This is the Lord's way of verifying that sanctity is not something abstract and esoteric. Rather, holiness is real and concrete; it can be experienced and accounted. But what are the criteria to use in judging the holiness of another? The answer is the Beatitudes.

We can tell if others are holy if they are in touch with their radical nothingness. They are "poor" of the delusion of ever mistaking what they have with who they are. They realize that they have no right ever to approach God except in explicit grace-filled acceptance of their abject nothingness — their unremitting destitution apart from grace. This remains a cause of great rejoicing for the saint.

Moreover, saints are ever mindful that they compound the essential poverty of the Christian life through choices, actions, and omissions that are sinful. True saints never lose sight of their real sinfulness, about which they remain duly sorrowful. For saints can never forget that Christ came to save the sick, and not the self-righteous. And although human beings live with the inescapable potential to sin, the Gospel fills saints with the confidence to believe that grace can and does perfect nature in the human being's ongoing process of becoming. This gives the saint a great sense of humor because the saint possesses a keen sensitivity to the ironic.

As a result, the saint lives emptied of self, renouncing any sense of entitlement. The humility, meekness, and lowliness famously associated with the saints is no false front; it is the only way to stay connected to and immersed in the milieu of "what really matters." For saints are supreme, sometimes even shocking, realists. They live the lowliness of spiritual childhood in order to root out any tendency to "live in denial" that might cunningly belittle them by giving them a false pretense for cottoning compromise or creating their own reality.

The saint's most fundamental longing is for ultimate communion with God. Saints hunger to be conformed to the Beloved. The more they come to terms with their emptiness and poverty, the more saints yearn to be filled only with what will satisfy and perfect them.

Forgiveness is the hallmark of the life of the saints because they recognize that everything they receive is the gift of the Father through the Passion of his Son. Therefore, as embodiments of the majesty of the Holy Spirit, saints are quick and relentless in extending compassion to the sinful, in saying "I'm sorry" for their own transgressions, and in granting forgiveness to anyone who offends them. It is easy and delightful to apologize to a saint. Saints personally manifest the beauty behind the *felix culpa*. They incarnate Love.

Saints live with undivided, pure hearts. They want only God and what God wants for them. They are happy to be detached or separated from anyone or anything that does not lead them into deeper union with God. Depending on our own disposition, this makes it either very easy or very difficult to live with them. Accordingly, saints relish friendship.

In terms of mission, the saint's life consists in reestablishing order and reconciliation in a chaos-filled world through their personal, vital friendship with the Holy Spirit. The peace that saints make transcends the world; it is the same peace issued by the risen Jesus.

And saints grow stronger, more peaceful and resolute when insulted, slandered, and persecuted because of their dedication to Jesus Christ — especially when it comes from others who share their religion. In fact, saints get worried when persecution lets up. A person whose life is surrounded with such unjust assault is quite likely on his way to sanctity.

ALL SOULS

TIME TO MEET ONE ANOTHER
John 14:1-6

The fact that Christ goes to prepare a place for us in his Father's house indicates that preparation for death is something we need to take seriously. We pray today for the holy souls in purgatory who are on their way to the heavenly dwelling place. As the Byzantine liturgy prays, "O Lord, in your goodness remember your servants and forgive every sin they have committed in their lives, for there is none without sin but yourself who have power to grant rest to the departed."

The night before he dies, Jesus expresses his desire that where he is we also may be. However, the realization of our everlasting communion with Christ depends on the genuineness of our devotion to Jesus – the Way, the Truth, and the Life. Through the seductive wiles of the world, we get lost on so many dead-end shortcuts, duped by so much masquerading deception, and dragooned by the culture of death. Hence, personal purification remains a prerequisite for entrance into heaven.

And yet, to be numbered among the holy souls is a cause of great joy. For those who populate purgatory are destined for heaven. That hope overshadows the pains of purification that the holy souls must undergo. This confidence led Cardinal John Henry Newman in a poem to extol purgatory as that sacred place "where hate, nor pride, nor fear torments / The transitory guest, / But in the willing agony / He plunges, and is blest."

Our prayer today for the holy souls in purgatory spurs us to reexamine the way we live our life on earth so as to make each moment a fitting preparation for the moment of death. St. Alphonsus Liguori counsels us that "those who expect death every hour will die a good death, even though it should come to them suddenly."

We need such constant vigilance, for the world is filled with countless alluring enticements that keep us from loving what we should. Reflecting on the venality of the world in a poem-prayer, Cardinal Newman wrote:

And thus, when we renounce for Thee
[The world's] restless aims and fears,
The tender memories of the past,
The hopes of coming years,
Poor is our sacrifice, whose eyes
Are lighted from above;
We offer what we cannot keep,
What we have ceased to love.

Indeed, it is only when we have ceased to love what is undeserving of our love, what is beneath our God-given dignity, that we are prepared to attain our destiny of heaven. For this reason, St. Thomas Aquinas observed that "the life of man consists in the affection which principally sustains him and in which he finds his greatest satisfaction." The quality of the love in our life determines the happiness of our death. Thus, by examining what we truly love, we discover if we are ready for heaven.

As a result, to enter into the ambience of heaven we must never leave the milieu of "what really matters." We may have to petition the blessed ones in heaven time and again each day to give us clarity about what really matters, for our understanding is weak and rebellious. The moment that we think we have it "all figured out" is the moment we need a radical reminder about what really matters: "No one comes to the Father except through me."

Are we truly living "in Jesus"? Even him we cannot know fully until our preparation is complete. In this regard, we do well humbly to remember the deathbed words of St. Teresa of Ávila, Doctor of the Church: "O my Lord and my Spouse, the hour that I have so desired has come. It's time for us to meet one another."

The Dedication of the Lateran Basilica

The Dedication that Rededicates Us
John 2:13-22

The travesty caused by the purveyors sullying the temple precincts stems from their obliviousness to the presence of the divine. The temple is not merely the Father's house; it is the very dwelling of God. The business people's mercenary interests betray their apathy at best and their disdaining dissent at worst. The immensity, grandeur, and beauty of the temple exist to stave off the trivializing inclinations of unredeemed humanity. God's majesty does not require such splendor. Rather, without such an ostensible reminder in our midst, the human spirit would cave in to pettiness and self-seeking. It is that irreligious disregard that Christ drives out of the temple.

This dynamic underlies today's feast of the dedication of the Basilica of St. John Lateran. As we celebrate the mother church of Christendom, we recall not simply the historical dedication of a sacred building but rather our own dedication to Holy Mother Church that the structure represents. The *Catechism* teaches us that the world was created for the sake of the Church (760), and that Christ and his Church together make up the "whole Christ" (795). Our meditation today on the Lateran basilica reminds us of our sacred vocation and dignity. In particular, three aspects of the Lateran basilica help us to renew our dedication to the whole Christ.

First of all, the chair from which the pope delivers *ex cathedra* statements is situated not in St. Peter's but in the Lateran basilica. Here five ecumenical councils were held. Here the great truths of the faith were propounded with conviction and courage. This feast of the Lateran reminds us of the fullness of the faith that fulfills our lives when we encounter so many swindlers and panderers who want to deceive us into believing that life can have meaning without God.

Moreover, attached to the Lateran basilica is the second-oldest baptistry on earth after the Jordan River. From this most holy font, the people who had been newly baptized at the Easter Vigil were led to the basilica at dawn to join the throngs of the faithful gathered as the *synaxis*, the sacred assembly, united in their participation at Easter Mass. The Lateran basilica is a perduring witness to the hope that should fill every Christian. For in every age, the ageless offer of salvation is made by the Church to those who yearn to escape the darkness of the world and to be raised up to a glory that surpasses even that of the original temple in Jerusalem.

And finally, in the Lateran basilica is an altar that contains a table on which every pope in the history of the Church has celebrated the Eucharist. The Lateran thereby assures us of the unending Communion that fills us, literally and figuratively, with the loving zeal that is all-consuming.

In reflecting upon his visit to the Lateran basilica, Dante wrote:

> If barbarians . . . were wonder-struck at such a spectacle,
> Imagine with what wonder I was filled,
> Who came from earthly things to things divine,
> From time unto eternity itself. . . .

As we celebrate the dedication of this great place, we remember that the basilica is dedicated to Christ the Savior. It is as we confess anew our need for such a Savior that we enter most ardently into this feast that rededicates us to our eternal destiny.

CONCLUSION
LECTIO DIVINA FOR PREACHING

In Georges Bernanos' *Diary of a Country Priest*, M. le Curé de Torcy says, "The Word of God is a red-hot iron. And you who preach it should go picking it up with a pair of tongs, for fear of burning yourself." How can a preacher effectively harness the fire of the Word of God without getting burnt himself? The answer is the Church's ancient practice of *lectio divina*.

WHAT IS *LECTIO DIVINA*?

Lectio divina refers to a special method of sacred reading – i.e., religious, dutiful listening to the Word of God that culminates in contemplation. The term *lectio* comes from the Latin verb *lego*, which refers to "tying together," "gathering up," and "harvesting." Mario Masini points out that "the end result ... lies above all in harvesting the messages, suggestions, and inspirations which are expressed by the sacred text and which we encounter there."

As Fr. Louis Bouyer understands it, *lectio divina* "is personal reading of the Word of God during which we try to assimilate its substance; a reading in faith, in a spirit of prayer, believing in the real presence of God who speaks to us in the sacred text, while the [reader] strives to be present in a spirit of obedience and total surrender to the divine promises and demands."

The living presence of God in Holy Writ is what makes *lectio divina* possible. "The text breathes," as poet and dramatist Paul Claudel put it. The in-spiration of *lectio divina* effects a personal encounter with Jesus Christ. Thus, it consists not so much in reading a book but in seeking Someone. A prior of the Camaldolese hermitage in Ohio once said to me, "A book is your friend." This is why Archbishop Mariano Magrassi counsels that, in undertaking *lectio divina*, "all our vital energies must come into play: understanding and its ability to penetrate in order to 'read within'; the will and its capacity for commitment; the heart and its ability

169

to react affectively; the imagination and its unlimited creative power in order to reconstruct events." *Lectio divina* takes us beyond the superficial and mediocre, and transports us into the heart of reality.

Hence, the objective of *lectio divina* is not simply to divine some new theological insight; that could cater to the worst kind of spiritual pride in the preacher. Rather, *lectio divina* is authentic if we approach the Word of God with the willingness to be changed, formed, and directed. To this end, St. Bernard admonishes, "Listen to the inner voice; use the eyes of your heart, and you will learn by experience."

There are four stages of *lectio divina*: *lectio, meditatio, oratio,* and *contemplatio.*

Lectio refers to the reader's reverent, attentive, profound, and devout listening to the Word of God. To be deeply appreciated and appropriated, the sacred text needs to be read and reread closely. Fr. Bouyer explains that "the idea is not to launch into a swift voyage of discovery, but to trace and retrace our path, to explore thoroughly, to make truly our own some part of the country hitherto known but superficially and assimilated imperfectly."

Meditatio (also called *ruminatio*) signifies the act of tasting and relishing the Word of God. As the *Catechism* expresses it:

> Meditation engages thought, imagination, emotion, and desire. This mobilization of faculties is necessary in order to deepen our convictions of faith, prompt the conversion of our heart, and strengthen our will to follow Christ. Christian prayer tries above all to meditate on the mysteries of Christ, as in *lectio divina* (2708).

In this second stage of *lectio divina*, the reader may employ the resources of biblical scholarship in order to pursue serious study of the Word's true meaning. In this way, *meditatio* seeks to identify the values, attitudes, and emotions communicated via the text.

With the third stage, *oratio*, the sacred reading becomes formal prayer. The *Catechism* teaches that "*lectio divina* [is] where the Word of God is so read and meditated that it becomes prayer" (1177). This prayer takes the form of a dialogue of love with the heavenly Father, for we need such a dialogue in order to know God as a Person. *Oratio*, then, is real conversation consisting of praise, thanksgiving, supplication, petitions, asking for forgiveness, and so on, whereby we express our faith as spiritual children of the Father.

Finally, through *contemplatio* we reach the ultimate goal of all *lectio divina*: contemplation that deepens our comprehension of the words and deeds of divine revelation. In this fourth stage, we are caught up in the Mystery of Christ, for in our reading we now grasp that the God of love is *seeking us* through our endeavor. *Contemplatio* enables us to delight in the personal bond we have with God. Fr. Bouyer describes it thus: "In every Word of God, what matters most is God's opening his own heart to us in it, and it is by this that our heart should be touched, changed from top to bottom. . . . This 'knowledge' is contemplation, the absorption of self in what we contemplate."

Canon Jacques Leclercq sums up *lectio divina* in this way: "The mouth pronounces the words of the text, the memory fixes them in the mind, the intelligence understands their significance, the will desires to translate them into works." And the ninth-century Benedictine monk Smaragdus adds this:

> When we read, it is God who speaks with us. . . . Reading enables us to learn what we do not know, meditation enables us to retain what we have learned, and prayer enables us to live what we have retained. Reading Sacred Scripture confers on us two gifts: it makes the soul's understanding keener, and after snatching us from the world's vanities, it leads us to the love of God.

WHY DO WE NEED *LECTIO DIVINA*?

If we are honest, we will acknowledge how much we are prejudiced, if not deluded, by our own opinions and self-judgments. How great is the temptation to rationalize the Word of God, accommodating it to justify our philosophical positions, our view of reality. And yet, as the gifts of the Holy Spirit attest, the Mystery of God is greater than human reason. Since the Truth cannot be reduced to the laws of our mind, the mind must not impose its constricted categories and stratagems on the Word.

The eleventh-century monk Berno of Reichenau warns, "Prudent reader, do not try to accommodate the Scriptures to your own meanings or add your own meanings to the Scriptures."

Moreover, as Fr. Michael Casey, O.C.S.O., aptly observes, "We have lost the skill of tracking through a complex argument to arrive at unassailable conclusions." However, without an appropriate sacred tenacity, we cannot reach the Bible's meaning, which can at times be puzzling and somewhat obscure. St. Gregory the Great notes that "when the sense of the Word of God seems to leave the one who reads it tepid, when the language of Scripture does not inflame his soul and does not cause some resplendent meaning to dance in his soul, even the 'wheels' remain inert on earth, because the living being does not rise from earth." The revelation of Sacred Scripture must be pursued voluntarily and passionately via a process that deeply engages our freedom.

Even more, as Fr. Casey continues, "we have not accepted the consequences of submitting the totality of our lives to progressive evangelization. We hope to keep intact a small portion of heathen territory where our private authority is unquestioned. In this case we seem to have forgotten the pithy saying attributed to St. John of the Cross: 'A bird can be as securely restrained by a light cord as by a stout chain.' " When confronted with the ultimate authority of the Word of God, we need a dynamic by which to abrogate our private authority and implicate ourselves in the saving truth of God's Word.

Lectio divina is the sacred strategy that delivers us from self-serving rationalizations, that revitalizes our powers of reason, and that recommits us in self-donation to the Gospel of Jesus Christ. Smaragdus states that "to experts, Sacred Scripture is revealed as ever new," and *lectio divina* is the system by which we access that newness. For as the twelfth-century theologian and mystic William of Saint-Thierry reminds us:

> The Scriptures need to be read and understood in the same
> spirit in which they were created. In all Scripture, diligent
> reading is as far from superficial perusal as friendship is
> distinct from acquaintance with a stranger, or as affection
> given to a companion differs from a casual greeting.

What Does *Lectio Divina* Do?

St. Gregory the Great underscores the invaluable effect of *lectio divina*:

> Often, through the grace of the almighty Lord, certain passages in the sacred text are better understood when the divine Word is read privately. The soul, conscious of its faults and recognizing the truth of what it has heard, is struck by the dart of grief and pierced by the sword of compunction, so that it wishes to do nothing but weep and wash away its stains with floods of tears.

Archbishop Magrassi suggests that "the Word reflects our image. It is the tool for a ruthless diagnosis of our life. It strips bare our secret thoughts and reveals to us our heart. It enables us to interpret our life, to read in the book of experience." In the phrasing of St. Athanasius: "The text becomes a mirror in which may be seen the movements of one's own soul."

In this light, we can appreciate the recommendation of St. John Cassian: "Each hour and every moment we keep opening the ground of the heart with the plow of the Gospel — that is, with the constant recalling of Christ's cross — and so we can eliminate the wounds inflicted by wild beasts and the bites of poisonous snakes." Accordingly, Smaragdus can rightly claim that *lectio divina* "sharpens perception, enriches understanding, rouses from sloth, banishes idleness, orders life, corrects bad habits, produces salutary weeping, . . . draws tears from contrite hearts, . . . curbs idle speech and vanity, and awakens longing for Christ and the heavenly homeland."

Thus, we experience *image-restoration* through the practice of *lectio divina* that returns divine transparency to our inner self. The eleventh-century mystic Simeon the New Theologian says that *lectio divina* "unlocks the coffers, manifests and renders visible and comprehensible things hidden and closed, unseals the Book, and gives the reader the sense of Scripture." Mystical writer Henry of Marcy informs us that "under the effect of the revealing action of the Spirit our spirit expands and is raised to a level where it can understand the Scriptures."

Through *lectio divina*, we gain the mind of Christ. *Lectio divina* remains an incomparable source of spiritual energy that effects in us an enhanced level of fervor and that breaks down the barriers between our fallible awareness and the Truth. It opens us to the action of grace and the promptings of the Holy Spirit in a way that surpasses the self-wrought perceptions and expectations that otherwise constrain us.

The lasting contact with the Word of God established by *lectio divina* empowers us to withstand the distraction and fragmentation that beset our lives. It motivates us to do God's will simply because it is good. It persuades without moralizing because, as Archbishop Magrassi explains, "morality is impoverished when it is divorced from mystery." *Lectio divina* invites God's Word to shape our beliefs and values so as to "evangelize our behavior," writes Fr. Casey. Mystical writer Gottfried of Admont wrote: "If we love to drink the wine of Sacred Scripture with our spiritual intelligence, we will know how to make of it our food through the understanding of our hearts, and will see arise over us the radiant morning of God."

At the same time, *lectio divina* contributes to our *image-perfection*. It blesses us with the fullness of God, increasing the likeness to the divine within us. St. Clement of Alexandria testifies, "Indeed, these letters must be sacred, for they make us not only holy but also divine." St. John Chrysostom hastens to explain that "even if the [scriptural] phrase is short, its power is great. Often, one word taken from there is enough to serve as viaticum for an entire lifetime." Moreover, as St. Gregory the Great asserts, "the divine words grow with one who reads them. . . . Where the mind of the reader is directed, there, too, the sacred text ascends; for . . . it grows with us, it rises with us." And Blessed Rabanus Maurus adds that "the higher you rise, the higher the divine Word rises with you." We know the godly effect of *lectio divina* when "the words of Scripture have ceased to be external; they have become ourselves," says Claudel.

How Do We Do Lectio Divina?

Here are seven steps (according to the classic four stages) for doing *lectio divina* in preparation for preaching:

I. Lectio

1. Early in the week (on Sunday or Monday) set aside one hour — preferably before the Blessed Sacrament — to do *lectio divina* of the

Sacred Scriptures for the coming Sunday liturgy. Since the Holy Spirit "disposes the one who reads to be obedient to the Word" (St. Gregory the Great), begin with a prayer to the Holy Spirit for illumination, such as the following:

Holy Spirit of Truth,
the Word of God creates in us
the capacity to receive the action
by which you apply the saving events of Jesus Christ
to our lives right now.
Make me open to that action.
Inspire my mind and illumine my heart
that I may pierce the pearl of this Holy Scripture
and penetrate the inner dimension of God's Word
so that events of the Redemption may reach me and my
     hearers
now by Word.

Be sure to pray the Scripture from *both* the Lectionary *and* the Bible itself so as to understand and appreciate the context of the given passage, its placement within the whole of the book, and how it connects with what precedes or follows it in the text. This obviates the danger of subjectivism in interpretation.

2. Pray the text aloud in order to benefit from the auricular reinforcement.

3. Actually write out the text according to units that are meaningful to you; make it fit on one sheet of paper that you can then work from. Inscribing the Scripture for ourselves saves us from merely scanning a well-known passage with our eyes. We begin to see connections, parallels, contrasts, inconsistencies, and other distinctive and conspicuous elements that might otherwise go unnoticed. The act of writing engages a deep part of our consciousness and unleashes the creative process. As Fr. Casey notes:

The act of writing is itself a meditation — a way of assimilating what we read. We write carefully and reverently as a

175

means of staying longer with the text and exploring its implications. As we do it, the word is imprinted more fully on our consciousness and there is a greater possibility that it will continue to exercise an influence over us in the future.

By writing, the Word becomes our own.

II. Meditatio

4. Be sensitive to anything that moves or intrigues you — no matter what or why. Mark anything on that sheet that strikes you — e.g., unusual words, repetitions, patterns, verbs, proper nouns, adjectives, and adverbs that modify and color your interpretation — anything that piques your interest, your emotions, or that causes you to wonder, and so on. Be especially mindful of questions that are posed in the text; you can be certain that they are intended for readers of every age to answer. All these things can be examined with the assistance of a good concordance or an encyclopedia of biblical theology.

III. Oratio

5. Ask in prayer: "What's in this for me? What does this Scripture promise? How can this Scripture concretely change my life?" Fr. Bouyer emphasizes:

> What is said to us is the Word of God: in fact, it is God who speaks to us, who never ceases to speak to us in these words. Even though they have been fixed in their phrasing for thousands of years, he who makes us hear them today already had us in mind when he inspired them of old, and he is always present to address himself to us through them, as if they were at this instant pronounced for the first time.

St. Gregory the Great assures us that "all Scripture was written for us. . . . When the reader addresses a question to the text, the answer is in proportion to the reader's maturity."

IV. Contemplatio

6. Prayerfully fix your heart on this question: "What does this Scripture reveal about Jesus Christ?" The medieval mystic Hugh of St. Victor reminds us that "all Sacred Scripture is but one book, and this one book is Christ; because all Sacred Scripture speaks of Christ, and all Sacred Scripture is fulfilled in Christ." Fr. Casey directs us to "dialogue with the text as though it were a person, asking it questions and listening for responses within." As Archbishop Magrassi maintains, "Until I speak to God and God speaks to me, even though I might know everything about God, God is not a person for me. Once God speaks to me, God becomes a 'thou' whom I address. At that precise moment authentic personal relationship begins." Pope Paul VI encouraged, "Never tire as you strive to elicit from the depths of your soul and with your inner voice this 'THOU!' addressed to the ineffable God, that mysterious Other who sees us, waits for us, loves us."

7. Pray and share the fruits of meditation regarding Scripture with others. Fr. Casey interjects, "The Bible is addressed not to me as an individual but as a member of the Church. Often a hidden meaning will be unveiled by recourse to a brother or sister."

In short, as Fr. Bouyer advises, "while reading, we should be all adherence, all abandonment, all self-donation, in . . . faith, to what we hear and to him whom we hear behind the words being read or reread."

RESOURCES

The various citations in this chapter were taken from the following sources, which are excellent resources for further study of *lectio divina*:

- Bouyer, Louis. *Introduction to Spirituality*. New York: Desclee, 1961.
- Casey, Michael. *Sacred Reading: The Ancient Art of Lectio Divina*. Liguori, Mo.: Triumph, 1995.
- Leclercq, Jacques. "*Lectio Divina*," in *DIP*, Vol. V, Rome 1978, pp. 561-66.
- Magrassi, Mariano. *Praying the Bible: An Introduction to Lectio Divina*. Collegeville, Minn.: Liturgical Press, 1998.

- Masini, Mario. *Lectio Divina: An Ancient Prayer That Is Ever New.* New York: Alba House, 1998.
- Panimolle, Salvatore A., ed. *Like the Deer That Yearns: Listening to the Word and Prayer*. Petersham: St. Bede's Publications, 1998.

Don't be afraid of the effort that *lectio divina* requires; it's worth it! As M. le Curé de Torcy concludes, "When the Lord has drawn from me some word for the good of souls, I know because of the pain of it."

Index

Entries for such words as *Jesus Christ, Church,* and *God,* which appear on almost every page of the text, are listed with the first page on which the word occurs followed by "*et passim.*" Except for some entries that have been modified, most references are to the pages on which the word appears, rather than to those on which the topic is discussed. Thus, when a word has more than one meaning (for instance, *Communion*), all meanings are listed together.

Blasphemy, 113, 119
Bless, 28, 141
Blessed Sacrament, 84, 174
Blessing, 14, 29, 76, 127, 130, 162
Blind, 25, 37, 43-44, 59-60, 66, 85-86, 105, 109, 114, 134
Bliss, 63
Blood, 14, 59, 83, 93
Blood of Christ, 59, 83, 126
Boat, 39, 103-104
Body, 31, 38, 47, 55, 65, 72, 74, 79-80, 84, 88, 123, 145-146, 157-160
Body of Christ, 14, 31, 55-56, 65, 83-84, 96, 135, 160
Bond, 119, 171
Borrower, 47
Bouyer, Louis, 169-171, 176-177
Boy, 86, 105, 109, 148
Brainwash, 97
Branches, 162
Bravado, 127
Bride, 28
Bridegroom, 41, 121, 129-130
Brilliance, 55-56
Brother, 29, 156, 177
Berno of Reichenau, 172
Brutality, 119
Burden, 76, 89, 94, 161-162
Bury, 29, 51
Byzantine, 56, 63, 165
Caananite, 86
Caesar, 123
Calamity, 120
Call, 15, 21-22, 49, 53, 70, 72, 93-94, 104, 107-108, 135
Calvary, 42, 56, 61, 64, 90, 110, 126
Cana, 37
Capacity, 13-14, 89, 155, 169, 175
Capernaum, 39, 85, 123
Car, 83
Care, 22, 48, 53, 67, 119, 135
Career Choice, 74
Carpenter, 40
Cartesian Formula, 108
Casey, Michael, 15, 172, 174-175, 177
Cassian, St. John, 173
Catalyst, 53, 112
Catechism of the Catholic Church, 14, 23, 27, 31, 33-34, 67-68, 73, 78, 84, 91, 154, 167, 170
Catherine of Siena, St., 56, 162
Catholic, 14, 88, 91, 142
Cause, 16, 43-44, 49, 98, 139, 163, 165, 172
Cemetery, 65
Center, 33, 55, 88
Centerpiece, 145
Centurion, 85, 114
Chain, 172
Chance, 54, 100, 116, 120, 124, 131, 139
Change, 13, 68, 82, 91, 117-118, 158, 176

Character, 11, 15, 92, 99, 126, 129
Characteristics, 84
Charity, 14, 42, 45, 78, 98, 112, 162
Chesterton, G.K., 32
Chicanery, 124
Chief Priests, 103, 115
Child, 23, 27, 34, 79, 120, 142-143, 145-146, 159
Choice, 49, 74
Christian, 14-15, 43, 49, 64, 67, 77, 94, 112, 115, 123, 128, 134, 153-154, 163, 168, 170
Christmas, 21, 27, 31, 141-143
Chrysostom, St. John, 61-62, 174
Church, 12, *et passim*
Circumstance, 40, 97
Civil, 123
Clarity, 55, 150, 166
Claudel, Paul, 169, 174
Clay, 59
Clean, 41, 46, 88, 139
Cleansing, 73, 88
Clement of Alexandria, St., 174
Cleverness, 129
Climax, 37, 70
Cloak, 47, 114
Clothing, 65
Cloud, 40, 55, 75, 147
Clue, 104, 131
Coexist, 96
Collateral, 100, 132
Coming, 21, 24, 28, 31, 35, 37-38, 48, 94, 166, 175
Command, 27, 65, 85, 88, 92, 99, 101, 104, 113
Commission, 41, 111, 115, 151
Commitment, 124, 169
Commitment, 124, 169
Communicate, 22, 55, 144
Communion, 25, 44, 52, 58-59, 62, 64, 73-74, 80, 83, 89, 91, 94, 111, 146-147, 153-154, 160, 162-163, 165, 168
Community, 29, 87, 114
Companion, 39, 172
Compassion, 37, 51, 77, 87, 90, 114, 121, 139, 164
Complaining, 90
Comprehension, 11, 139, 171
Compromise, 41, 54, 74, 99, 153, 163
Compunction, 173
Conception, 30, 65, 111, 139-141, 150
Concrete, 23, 78, 80, 111, 113, 146, 163
Concupiscence, 56
Condemnation, 37
Condition, 26, 55, 84, 135, 149
Conduct, 11, 110, 160
Confession, 16, 57, 108, 111
Confidence, 28, 38, 53, 58, 80, 88, 98, 100, 103, 106, 109, 124, 127, 132, 151, 163, 165
Confirmation, 25, 64, 85, 130, 153

Conflict, 53, 85, 96, 149-150, 161
Conformity, 23, 37, 43, 91, 135, 145, 154
Connectedness, 83
Connection, 75, 159
Conniving, 123
Conscientiousness, 130
Consecration, 15
Consent, 64, 149
Consolation, 11, 45, 64, 94, 108, 162
Conspiracy, 124
Constancy, 45, 82
Contact, 15, 55, 58, 65, 88, 159, 174
Contemplatio, 170-171, 177
Context, 75, 175
Contingency, 82
Continuation, 65
Contradiction, 29
Convenience, 57
Conversation, 13, 171
Conversion, 14, 39, 57-58, 170
Conviction, 58, 69, 81, 159, 167
Cooperation, 57
Copper, 96
Cord, 172
Cornerstone, 120
Corporeality, 79
Corpus Christi, 83
Correction, 111-112
Corruption, 21, 141
Council, 115, 123
Counsel, 30, 73, 111, 141
Country, 33-34, 39, 169-170
Courage, 79, 107-108, 167
Cousin, 101
Covenant, 14, 75, 121
Covetousness, 75
Create, 13-14, 158, 160
Creation, 31, 59, 77, 81, 157-158
Creator, 81, 148
Credit, 139-140
Creed, 88, 91
Crippled, 44
Criteria, 97, 163
Criticism, 124
Cross, 15, *et passim*
Crowd, 37, 87
Crucifix, 161
Crucifixion, 37, 47, 63, 92, 121, 132
Culpability, 111
Cure, 66, 83, 109, 116
Cyril of Alexandria, St., 79
Dante, 168
Darkness, 31, 44, 65, 89-90, 93, 115, 122, 130, 168
Daughter, 29, 39, 79, 105-106, 122
David, King, 106
Dawn, 115, 168
Deacon, 14
Dead, 25, 65, 71, 83, 88, 154
Deaf, 25
Dealing, 48, 53, 116
Death, 11, *et passim*

182

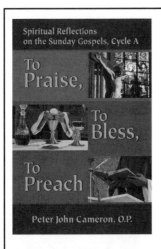
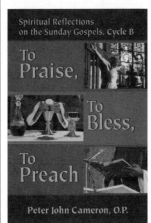
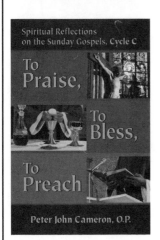

OUR SUNDAY VISITOR . . .
YOUR SOURCE FOR DISCOVERING
THE RICHES OF THE CATHOLIC FAITH

Our Sunday Visitor has an extensive line of materials for young children, teens, and adults. Our books, Bibles, booklets, CD-ROMs, audios, and videos are available in bookstores worldwide.

To receive a FREE full-line catalog or for more information, call **Our Sunday Visitor** at 1-800-348-2440. Or write, **Our Sunday Visitor** / 200 Noll Plaza / Huntington, IN 46750.

Please send me: ___A catalog
Please send me materials on:
___Apologetics and catechetics ___Reference works
___Prayer books ___Heritage and the saints
___The family ___The parish
Name_____
Address_____Apt._____
City_____State_____Zip_____
Telephone (   ) _____

A19BBABP

Please send a friend: ___A catalog
Please send a friend materials on:
____Apologetics and catechetics ____Reference works
____Prayer books ____Heritage and the saints
____The family ____The parish
Name_____
Address_____Apt._____
City_____State_____Zip_____
Telephone (   ) _____

A19BBABP

Our Sunday Visitor
200 Noll Plaza
Huntington, IN 46750
Toll free: **1-800-348-2440**
E-mail: osvbooks@osv.com
Website: www.osv.com